IS THE END NEAR???

Dr. Gene Schuyler

IS THE END NEAR???

IS THE END NEAR???
Published by Rebecca Publications

Copyright © 2020 by Gene Schuyler
Second Printing 2021
ISBN: 978-0-9908873-2-4

Cover design by: Marie Schuyler

Scripture quotations are from:
The Holy Bible, King James Version (KJV) unless otherwise stated.

Printed in the United States of America

ALL RIGHTS RESERVED
No part of this publication may be reproduced, stored in a retrieval system or transmitted in any form by any means - electronic, mechanical, photocopy, recording or otherwise - without prior permission of the publisher, except as provided by USA copyright law.

For information:
REBECCA PUBLICATIONS
1000 BAKERTOWN ROAD
FUQUAY-VARINA, NC 27526

PREFERENCE

When I began this series of messages at Mid-Way Baptist church, I knew that the Bible gives us information of how the beginning of the end would be; but, in 2020, in my life time, I now see how close we are to the return of Jesus Christ.

As of this date, March 31, 2020, my wife and I are complying with the stay-at-home order imposed by our Governor of North Carolina because of the Coronavirus. We could be under this order for 30 to 60 days.

The whole world is facing and going through one, if not the worse situation it has ever faced since the beginning of time. It is under a pandemic disease that is taking lives by the thousands as I write this, it is called "a pandemic disease." New York is the epic center of the virus with more cases and deaths than any other state in America. Hospital ships have been brought in for two states, New York and Louisiana. Emergency Rooms have also been erected in Central Park in New York and other facilities to accommodate the sick. This is just a beginning!!!

At the time of this writing and before the publication of this book, let me just say that this virus in the world today may not be tied to our Lord's judgment of sin on this world and mankind, for I know we must be careful what I say, but remember, Jesus referred to these times in His teachings found in Luke chapter 21 and the book of the Revelation chapters 11 and 16.

Let me say this as a preface to the study. The second coming of Jesus Christ in the Bible is very clear on its prophecy.

IS THE END NEAR???

It tell us how it will be in this world just prior to His return for His church. I see even more of an urgency than ever before to have this book published.

    May God bless each of you that reads this book and shares the soon return of our Savior with your family, friends and co-workers the wonderful gospel of Jesus Christ.

DEDICATION

     In giving these messages to the good people of the Mid-Way Baptist Church in Raleigh, North Carolina, during the Sunday evening services, to them all, thanks. I also dedicate this book to my wonderful wife, Marie, for her dedication and her walk with her Savior as a supportive wife, mother and Bible teacher.

     A grateful heart goes out to our dear friend Judy Naylor who has stood by us in critiquing every book God has given me the priviledge to write. Also, for Roger Naylor, her husband, who allowed Judy to give of her time and service to our Lord!

INTRODUCTION

PROPHECY AND THE BOOK OF REVELATION

"Escape from the coming night."

GETTING EXCITED ABOUT JESUS COMING!! EXPLANATION AS TO WHY STUDY PROPHECY AND THE BOOK OF REVELATION....A well-known preacher from the past said, "Start slow, go slow, rise higher and then catch fire."

The book of the Revelation is the last book in the Word of God and perhaps the most important book of all. It is supposed to be very "figurative," "symbolical," "hidden," "veiled," and "secret." Well, that is not so! Revelation is one of the plainest books in the Bible, but the problem folks have with this book is that it is hard to believe.

The writer of the book was the Apostle John, who also was the author of the Gospel of John and the three epistles in the New Testament.

This form of theology simply means that Jesus Christ will come back to this earth before the one thousand years.

AUTHOR'S FORWARD

Is the end near for this world? The entertainment industry and television gives all kinds of movies showing how it will be when the "WORLD COMES TO AN END." With their movies of a worldwide plague or maybe some global catastrophe happening, at least for those who have no idea or knowledge of what it will be like; the entertainment industry does not give the true picture or say what the true outcome will be.

For the Christian, and those who are asking the questions, in this book I take you through the book of Revelation proving that the end of this world will be anything but dreadful for the Christian. In fact, it should be something that every Christian should look forward to and encourage each of us to be ever mindful that the "End is Near" and to be ever helping family, friends and co-workers with the question - - "are you ready to meet God?" Why? Because God has told us the world will end. He has assured us that the end of this age will mark the beginning of a new and wonderful world and a glorious beginning where each of those born again, those who have trusted Christ as their personal Savior, will one day serve and worship our Lord Jesus in sinless perfection and where our eternal hope, as believers, is tied to the end of this world.

IS THE END NEAR???

    I have tried, in these series of messages, through the wonderful book of Revelation to show just how close this world is seeing the second coming of Christ. Not only is Revelation the inspired Word of God, but it is also the only New Testament book that includes a promised spiritual blessing for those who study and apply its message. As such, it is an essential part of every Christian's devotional life. Those who ignore Revelation deprive themselves of a rich treasure of divine truth, and the promised blessings that come from understanding that truth.

    It is my hope that it will give the reader a new conception of Christ and a new understanding of what it means to be working for our Savior while there is time to warn the lost to come to Jesus.

Gene Schuyler

Table of Contents

Preference V
Dedication VII
Introduction VIII
Author's Forward IX

Chapter One
    Prophecy and the book of Revelation 13

Chapter Two
    The Mysteries and Wonders of Prophecy 21

Chapter Three
    Four Terrible Horsemen 35

Chapter Four
    Angels of Doom - More Information 54

Chapter Five
    When All Hell Breaks Loose 73

Chapter Six
    Earth's Last Trial 80

Chapter Seven
    One Thousand Years of Peace 95

Chapter Eight
    The City of Glory - Revelation 21 109

Chapter Nine
    Where is Israel in Bible Prophecy 143

Chapter Ten
    Revelation of the Man of Sin or Satan's Superman 166

Student Worksheets 189

Conclusion 223

CHAPTER ONE

PROPHECY AND THE BOOK OF REVELATION

IS THE END NEAR???

*N*ow that you have read the introduction we will begin this study. We want to take a little while to look at the author, THE APOSTLE JOHN and notice something about how John writes.

1. John speaks as a zoologist: First of all Jesus is seen as a LAMB and as a LION. Then as we go into the Revelation we will see that there are those that are referred to as an OX, EAGLE, LAMB, A BEAST OUT OF THE SEA.

2. John speaks as an astronomer: He says, "Jesus holds seven stars in his hand---he says Satan sweeps the stars from heaven."

3. He speaks as an artist: Paints of colors: white many times over and over, i.e. white horses, robes, Jesus is seen dressed in white linen(purity) the Great White

CHAPTER ONE

Throne, green-emerald, i.e. Life. He then sees four horsemen: black = famine; gray = death; red = war; woman purple = richness and loyalty.

4. He speaks as a geographer: woman = 7, mountains = Rome, sea = peoples and nations, crystal river = blessings of God.

5. He speaks as a mathematician: 7 spirits — so many 7's mentioned in this study.

7 churches, 7seals, 7 vials,

7 judgments, and 7 persons.

Now here is a good question. How do we interpret this book — literally or symbolically? BOTH! HOW?

Well, Satan is a great red dragon! When you find out what the symbol is - then you see it as literal - for Satan is real!! Then there is the Woman on the 7 hills - symbol, literal it is Rome.

Symbolism of Numbers and their Meaning:

#1 is the number of unity and the nature of God: Deuteronomy 6:4; Zechariah 14:9; Ephesians 4:4-6 and the number one is the number of beginnings.

#2 is the number of witness: John 8:17 "second the motion." Jesus is the second person in the Trinity: 2 angels at the tomb of Jesus' resurrection and the number two is also the number of separation.

#3 is the Divine number: Trinity or three in one; Revelation 1:8; Matthew 28:19; Isaiah 6:3. Man is three: body, soul and spirit. Jesus rose on the 3rd day.

IS THE END NEAR???

#4 is the earth number: Creation - Isaiah 11:12; 4 corners of the earth (North, East, South and West) and 4 seasons (Summer, Spring, Fall and Winter).

#5 is the number for testing, as well as the number 10.

#6 is man's number.

#7 is God's number of completion: notice:

- ❖ 7 years of plenty
- ❖ 7 years of famine
- ❖ 7 years Nebuchadnezzar was insane
- ❖ 7 Beatitudes
- ❖ 7 petitions in the Lord's prayer
- ❖ 7 times Jesus spoke from the cross
- ❖ 7 churches in John's day
- ❖ 7 basic divisions of church history
- ❖ 7 characteristics can exist in any body of believers
- ❖ 7 golden candlesticks
- ❖ 7 angels (pastors)
- ❖ Over 44 times in the book of Revelation the number 7 occurs.

#8 is the number for "new beginnings". . Noah the eighth person.

So then, we need to conclude that every word, every statement, every symbol is relevant and has a definite meaning.

Well, the principle upon which this verse-by-verse study of Revelation proceeds, is that the contents of the book are, in the main, yet future and that the fulfillment of the greater part of Revelation cannot take place as long as the Church remains here on earth.

CHAPTER ONE

When the Lord Jesus comes in the Rapture, and the Church is caught up to meet Him in the air, then the events in Revelation from chapter 4 through chapter 22 will occur! Watch this now: The New Testament Church is now in the process of being called out and will be completed when the Rapture occurs. This is known as the Church Age — or the Dispensation of Grace. But after the Rapture of the 17 week of Daniel's prophecy (Daniel 9:27), will bring about startling changes here on this earth.

The events recorded in chapters 4 and following cannot take place as long as the Church is here on earth.

Evil is certainly present and actively at work, and the mystery of iniquity is already working----BUT the mystery of iniquity is restrained, kept in check, by the HOLY SPIRIT (II Thessalonians 2:6-7). As we study this book, let me also join with John in saying.....O K, WHAT DOES REVELATION MEAN?

WHAT DOES REVELATION MEAN? "**THE VEIL ROLLED ASIDE**"

The visions recorded in this book were seen by John on the Isle of Patmos and written about the year of our Lord 96 A.D. and it has three divisions.

This threefold division is found in chapter 1:19 and this verse unlocks the interpretation and the understanding of Revelation. Verse 19 speaks of the past, present and the future.

As we study this book, we find that there is a key verse and the key is hanging at the very entrance of the book as it is true of the book of Revelation. Notice:

1. "Write - the things which thou hast seen." What John had just seen is recorded in verses 10-18. Here Christ is in the

midst of the seven golden candlesticks which is the central object of these verses and this is past tense.

2. "Write the things - which are." The things are recorded in chapters 2 and 3.

3. "Write the things - which shall be hereafter." Or, the things which will happen after the church age. At this present age we are living between Revelation 3:7 and 3:20. There are 12 distinct sections in the book of Revelation:

   1. Chapter 1:1-9 is the Introduction.

   2. Chapter 1:10-18: We see Christ in the midst of the seven golden candlesticks which represent the churches of Asia.

   3. Chapters 2 and 3: We will see the Church - God's witness on earth - growing in its departure from truth and its first love, moving farther and farther from God until the Laodiceans are spewed out of His mouth and the true believers at Philadelphia are caught out to meet the Lord in the air.

   4. Chapters 4 and 5: We will see the saints enthroned and glorified.

   5. Chapters 6:1-8:1: We learn of the seven seals opened by the Lamb.

   6. Chapters 8-9 and chapter 11:15-19: We will see the seven trumpets which are sounded by the seven angels.

   7. Chapters 12-14: We see two actors and in chapter 13 we see the seven outstanding results of their actions.

CHAPTER ONE

8. Chapters 15-16: We will study the seven vials of wrath poured out upon the earth.

9. Chapters 17-18: This deals with Babylon, both political and ecclesiastical.

10. Chapters 19-21:8: Has to do with the events from the fall of Babylon.

11. Chapters 21:9-22:5: We will study the Bride of the Lamb (the New Testament church).

12. Chapter 22:6-21: We will find the warning, threatenings, encouragements and the last prayer recorded in God's Word.

IS THE END NEAR???

THOUGHTS:

_____

_____

_____

_____

_____

_____

_____

ACTIONS:

_____

_____

_____

_____

_____

CHAPTER TWO

IS THE END NEAR???

MYSTERIES AND WONDERS OF PROPHECY

IS THE END NEAR???

The book of Revelation is one of the most amazing books of the Bible. Many pastors and teachers view this book as mystic and difficult to understand and as a result avoid its study altogether. Yet, it is a book of the Bible that nearly all biblical students desire to study and know. The fascination with the book of Revelation is based in its prophetic content, which mixes subterfuge with victory and triumph. Most people desire to know what the future has in store and the book of Revelation offers both hope and despair for the future. While many love to study Bible prophecy and the book of Revelation, there are others who hate this revealing text. Adrian Rogers once stated,

"There is someone who hates the books. His name is Satan. In fact, there are two books in the Bible Satan especially hates—Genesis and Revelation, the first and last books of God's Word."

❖ Why does Satan hate these two books? In the book of Genesis, Satan's doom is prophesied. In the book of

CHAPTER TWO

Revelation, Satan's doom is realized. There is no devil in the first two chapters of God's Word or in the last two chapters of God's Word. For every child of God, these are books that tie the gospel message together.

- In Genesis we see the creation of the heavens and the earth.
- In Revelation we see the creation of the new heavens and new earth.
- In Genesis we see the first Adam reigning on earth.
- In Revelation we see Jesus, the last Adam, reigning in glory. In Genesis we see an earthly bride brought to the first Adam. In Revelation we see a heavenly bride brought to the Lord Jesus Christ, the last Adam.
- In Genesis we see the beginning of death and the curse.
- In Revelation the Savior brings us to a state where there is no more death and no more curse.
- In the book of Genesis man is driven from God's face in sin. In the book of Revelation we see God's face in glory.
- In Genesis, Satan appears for the first time. In Revelation he appears on earth for the last time.
- "The book of Revelation is the golden clasp that seals God's Word in holy, divine perfection." Adrian's words are insightful and revealing.
- It seems to me that many who despise this book of the Bible hate it for the same reasons that Satan hates this text. If the prophecies in the Revelation are true, then it will scare the rebellion out of the lost and will provide an immovable foundation for the redeemed. These will be the results that we hope to discover as a result of this study; that the lost might be saved,

IS THE END NEAR???

and the saved might be secured with an undeniable assurance for the future.

Without any doubt in the study of Bible prophecy there is a security, purity, and liberty. Security is found through the inevitable conclusion discovered at the end of the study. Our Lord Jesus Christ wins over every evil foe and this corrupt creation and all those who choose to side with and serve Him are guaranteed the benefits of His glorious victory.

Our purity results from the anticipation and immanency of our Lord's rapture of His Church to begin the fulfillment of each of the end time events revealed through our Lord's prophetic Word (1 John 3:1-3).

Our liberty endures through the certain knowledge that though the enemies of our Lord may take our mortal lives through persecution, our eternal souls are secure and our physical resurrection is promised. We are truly free from the wickedness that surrounds us and the death that pursues us. Eternity is ours and our hope is lively and sure.

As far as I am concerned, far too long we have taught Christians to approach the Bible with a light heartedness.

We teach for life change and to reach a lost and dying world. The world is best evangelized by the members of the Church. How can our fellow Christians reach the world for Christ if they cannot remember the things they have studied beyond the door of the worship center or classroom. I believe that it is time to expect far more from our fellow Christians. A lost world demands it.

As you study this book, our prayer is that you will discover the mysteries and wonder revealed in the Revelation of our Lord Jesus Christ as given to the Apostle John.

CHAPTER TWO

As we begin the study in the Book of Revelation and Prophecy - there are some basic things that we must initially consider.

There are various points of view when it comes to the study of the Book of Revelation. Before we consider the various points of view there are some terms that need to be defined.

1. **Important Terms**

   a. <u>The Tribulation Period</u> – A period of time, lasting seven years, unlike any other period of time in human history where in the creation is redeemed by God through justice and judgment and wherein the antchrist, Satan's superman, is given unfettered authority over this corrupt world.

   b. <u>Rapture</u> – The taking out of those spiritually redeemed, also known as the Church of Jesus Christ, i.e., the "born again."

   c. <u>Post Tribulation</u> – A position that teaches that the rapture occurs after the seven year tribulation period.

   d. <u>Mid Tribulation or Pre-Wrath</u> – A position that teaches that the rapture occurs in the middle of the tribulation period.

   e. <u>Pre-Tribulation</u> – A position that teaches that the rapture occurs prior to the tribulation period. This view is what I consider correct and our church believes and will be the position held throughout this study.

f. **Millennium** – A period of one thousand years following the tribulation period and the second advent of Christ wherein our Lord Jesus Christ will reign supreme on this earth.

2. **Common Views**

Having considered the important terms we will now consider the various points of view employed when studying The Revelation or Bible Prophecy.

Understanding each of these viewpoints will help you to understand what a preacher, teacher, or fellow Christian means when they talk about various Bible prophecies. Altogether there are:

a. The Preterist School - The Preterist believes that the prophecies contained within Revelation have already been fulfilled. These commonly teach that everything contained in the book of Revelation found fulfillment when Israel was conquered by Titus in 70 A.D. Some might push the date of Israel's destruction back to 313 A.D., but the argument is essentially the same. The preterist teaches that we are not looking for a rapture, tribulation period, the millennial reign of Christ, and for some the second advent of Christ. Some preterist will go as far as to imply that we are currently living on the New Heaven and New Earth. In considering the pretenses of preterism it seems reasonable to imply that preterism is a form of Amillenialism which iterally mean "no millennium."

CHAPTER TWO

b. The Presentist School - Some refer to this as the Idealist or Allegorical View. "A Presentist is one who views the events in Revelation, not as actual events 'per se', but rather as an expression of those principles and forces active in any age." For instance, a presentist would imply that the Book of Revelation portrays the struggle between good and evil in our lives. To hold this position one would have to hold that the message in Revelation is allegorical in nature and is not intended to be understood in any literal sense.

c. The Progressive School - Also referred to by some as The Historical View. This view holds that Revelation presents the historic struggle of the Church as it has occurred throughout this current Church age. This point of view gained popularity during the beginning of the reformation but faded into oblivion when the 1260 day-year time period, essential to its understanding, expired without the anticipated fulfillment of its prophecy.

d. The Prophetic School - Often called the 'Futurist School'. The Futurist believes that the majority of Revelation is prophetic, and is yet to be fulfilled. The Futurist looks for the Rapture of the Church, the Bema Seat of Christ, and the Marriage Supper of the Lamb.

e. The Great Tribulation Period, the Second Advent of Christ, the Millennial Reign of Christ, the Great White Throne of Judgment, and the New Heaven and New Earth are all yet to come. All of these will be addressed as this study proceeds through the Revelation of our Lord Jesus Christ.

IS THE END NEAR???

So far we have looked at: Important Terms, Common Views, now:

3. **Their Implications** - Thus the question arises, "Does one's point of view really matter? Without any doubt one's point of view makes all the difference in the world. One's point of view will change the way they approach every other passage in the Word of God. Biblically and theologically ones point of view - **when it comes to Bible prophecy** - will change their whole understanding of the Bible. Your point of view will affect you.

4. **Interpretation or Hermeneutics** - Your point of view determines whether your normal approach to Scripture is allegorical or literal in nature which in turn will dictate your understanding of every other passage of Scripture.

    ❖ The pre-millennial, pre-tribulation, literal approach to the Bible will lead one to understand the Bible in its grammatical and contextual senses and will lead one to understand the remnant of the redeemed.

    ❖ The post or amillennial, mid or post tribulation approach largely allegorizes and manipulates various texts, often encouraging the understanding of texts outside of their context, especially in the parables and will lead one to be ecumenical in their understanding of the redeemed.

5. **Anticipation or Immanency**

    ❖ The pre-tribulationist and literalist will hold a sense of immanency concerning the near rapture of the

CHAPTER TWO

Church which will compel them to live in continuous preparation and purity.

❖ The post-millennialist or amillennialist will likely sense that, considering the world's current condition, that there is much time remaining and no need to be overly zealous about the Lord's return.

6. **Mission or Purpose** -The pre-tribulationist will understand that lost souls have only a short time to respond to the gospel and will work diligently to win the lost to Christ.

❖ The post or amillennialist will likely feel that their task is to help improve upon our political, cultural, and social conditions and their purpose will be more humanitarian than evangelical in nature.

❖ These are but a few of the areas affected by one's point of view concerning bible prophecy which in reality reflects ones point of view concerning Scripture all together. It is important to note that it is doctrinally impossible to be all things to all people when it comes to these points of view.

There is a term I call **"The Cooperation In View"** – The cooperation in view within the Revelation deals with the book's authorship. The epistle begins, **"The Revelation of Jesus Christ, which God gave unto him, to shew unto his servants things which must shortly come to pass; and he sent and signified it by his angel unto his servant John**" (Revelation 1:1). We notice immediately that this is not the Revelation of the Apostle John, it is the Revelation of

IS THE END NEAR???

Jesus Christ as given to the Apostle John. Hence, John is the penman that wrote the epistle, but our Lord Jesus Christ is the author of the book in that the text reveals Him in all His glory and the text was given through inspiration as is all scripture (2 Timothy 3:16-17).

It is true that the book of Revelation is often hard to understand. And many details won't become clear until these events begin to unfold, but God is not trying to conceal; He is trying to reveal.

Dr. Adrian Rogers explained that there is a key to help you unlock and understand this book. "It's hanging on the front door, in the first chapter, verse 19, within the Lord's commission to John to write this book." **"Write the things which thou hast seen, and the things which are, and the things which shall be hereafter"** (Revelation 1:19).

1. "Things you have <u>seen</u>."

    Jesus has come; He is the living, risen, resurrected Savior. What had John seen? A vision of the Lord Jesus Christ. Jesus said, **"Write it,"** and John wrote it. We could call this **"past things."** This division is small — only chapter one.

2. "Things which <u>are</u>."

    He is here now. Jesus is shown in the midst of the churches (chapters two and three). **"Where two or three are gathered together in My name, there am I in the midst of them"** (Matthew 18:20). *"The things which are"* refers to *"the Church Age,"* from Pentecost to the present. This division is also relatively small (only two chapters) and contains messages to seven churches.

CHAPTER TWO

While they were literal churches in Asia Minor back then, they also represent churches through the ages since. Right now we're living in *"the things which are."* We could call this **"present things."**

3. **"Things which shall be hereafter."**

   He is coming again. The remaining 19 chapters (the third division, Revelation 4-22) are prophecy, *"things which shall be hereafter."*

   "After this I looked, and, behold, a door was opened in heaven: And the first voice I heard…said, Come up hither, and I will show thee things which must be hereafter" (Revelation 4:1).

Only God knows the future. The devil doesn't. Nor do today's soothsayers, prophets, and prognosticators.

Understanding these three divisions is our golden key to Revelation, and with it on our hands we will be better equipped to understand.

As you study this book you are holding in your hand, devote your time to an in-depth study of the seven major events of Revelation.

1. **The Rapture of the Church/Departure of the Saints.** Notice that from Revelation 4:1 on, the word "church" drops out. Why? Because the church is going to be raptured. We who know Christ are not here on earth; we're in Heaven, experiencing the Judgment Seat of Christ and the Marriage of the Lamb (1 Thessalonians 4:16-18). When will the rapture take place? **At any moment. No sign or**

prophecy must yet be fulfilled before Jesus can come for His church.

2. **The Rise of the Beast/the Devil's Deceptions.** When the church is taken out, the man of sin, the antichrist, will be revealed (Revelation 13:1-3).

3. **The Great Tribulation/Devastation of the Earth.** For seven years the antichrist will hold sway, deceiving the nations, and God will pour out His wrath (Revelation 16-19).

4. **Armageddon/Defeat of the Beast and His Armies.** (Revelation 19:17-21).

5. **The Millenial Reign/Peace and Dominion of Jesus.** The lamb and lion will lie down together and Jesus will reign. (Revelation 20:1-6).

6. **The Final Judgment/Doom of the Lost.** *"And I saw a great white throne, and Him that sat on it...."* (Revelation 20:11-15).

7. **The Final State/Destiny of Mankind.** *"And He said unto me, it is done"* (Revelation 21:1-22:17).

CHAPTER TWO

Where Will You Be?

When God created you, He made you in His image, a living soul. Endless, timeless, dateless, measureless, your soul will be in existence somewhere. God is making new heavens and a new earth. When these things are going on, where will your soul be?

> **You have a life to live, a death to die, a judgment to face, and an eternity to endure, either in heaven or in hell.**

The wisest thing you could ever do would be to give your heart to Jesus Christ. The last words in the Bible are an invitation: *"And whosoever is athirst, let him come and take of the water of life freely."* And its last prayer is, *"Even so, come Lord Jesus."*

IS THE END NEAR???

THOUGHTS:

___

___

___

___

___

___

___

ACTIONS:

___

___

___

___

___

___

___

CHAPTER THREE

IS THE END NEAR???

FOUR TERRIBLE HORSEMAN

IS THE END NEAR???

Revelation Chapter 6:1-17

Quick review of the churches………Now then in the sixth chapter of Revelation it brings us to the beginning of the judgments of the wrath of God. It is not an easy passage to preach on, but it is part of the content of blessing promised to those who read and keep the prophecies of this book (Revelation 1:3).

If you live around here in North Carolina long enough you will get use to the summer months where we often experience sudden thunderstorms. Often before the storm there will be a strange calm, a sense of foreboding in the air. One could almost feel the violent storm that was about to break. **This is what we experience frequently in today's world.** There is a keen sense of an approaching crisis in the affairs of earth. Many secular writers of our day reflect this. To change the metaphor, it is as if we are floating down the stream of time and we sense that a great cataract is thundering ahead and we are about to plunge over the abyss.

CHAPTER THREE

The Bible has long predicted a crisis of that nature. One of the proofs that the Bible is from God is the fact that in the Old Testament the book of Daniel corresponds closely to the book of Revelation. Daniel saw many of the same things that John records here, although Daniel lived 500 years before John wrote. In the ninth chapter of his prophecy Daniel is given a great calendar that would outline history to its final days.

There was marked out a period of 70 "weeks," which means weeks of years. Seventy "weeks" times seven years is 490, so there would be 490 years that were to be fulfilled from the beginning of the building of the wall of Jerusalem in the days of Nehemiah, to the end of the age. **483 of those years would end on the day when the Messiah would be presented to Israel as her King.**

It is interesting that Sir Robert Anderson, head of Scotland Yard in Britain during the first part of the 20th century, carefully worked this out for us. **Watch this now:** "On the precise day when 483 years had run their course, Jesus rode down the Mount of Olives on a donkey and was presented to the nation as their King" (Daniel 9:25).

Just a few days later Christ was rejected and crucified, for the prophecy of Daniel had said that Messiah would be "cut off and have nothing," which is surely a reference to the crucifixion. After that there is an indeterminate, long-running period of time during which the prophet was told "wars and desolations were determined," (Daniel 9:26). It is during that indeterminate length of time that the church comes into being, starting on the Day of Pentecost when God began to call out a special people for his name, made up of both Jews and Gentiles. That church began over 2,000 years ago, and perhaps is almost completed now, but it is still on earth today. The prophet

IS THE END NEAR???

is then told of certain other events that were to occur **during the last seven years of that 490-year period.** Those events have not yet happened! Many commentators have thus understood that this seven-year period is still unfulfilled and when it begins it will be largely and closely associated with the nation of Israel.

Those seven years are referred to by Jesus himself in his great prophetic passage in Matthew 24. Before his crucifixion, as he sat on the Mount of Olives, he explained to the disciples what must come to pass. In that passage he refers several times to **"the end of the age,"** or more simply, **"the end."** That end is the seven-year period of Daniel's prophecy that will run its course when Israel is once again brought into prominence among the nations. It is that same period of seven years, which Revelation 6 through 19 covers, we are looking at the events to occur in that period. The four Gospels tell the story of the life of Christ, but one-third of the gospels focus upon the last week of our Lord, the seven days before the crucifixion. **Watch this now**-- Revelation 13, out of the 22 chapters, relates to the seven-year period of time which constitutes the end of the history of this age.

If you have read ahead a little in Revelation you will have noticed three series of events that occupy this last week of years.

▶▶ The first series is the seven seals, <u>six of which we will look at right now</u>. Included in the seals are seven trumpets that must yet sound, and seven bowls of wrath which are to be poured out upon the earth. Each of these series divides into four things and then three things:

▶▶ Four events that are outward, visible and easy to recognize, and then three revelations of what is going on behind the scenes, as it were, by the activity of angelic agencies, both for good and evil.

CHAPTER THREE

▶▶ Now let us look at the opening of the seven-sealed scroll which is held in the hands of the Lamb who was slain.

▶▶ John describes it in verses 1-2 of chapter 6--the word beasts is "zoon" which means "four living ones."
Look at chapter 4:7.

Lion: authority and power—the **majesty** of Jesus Christ.

Calf: **servitude** and sacrifice—the **ministry** of Jesus Christ.

Man: the **humanity** of the Lord Jesus Christ.

Eagle: the **deity** of the Lord Jesus Christ.

These four living creatures are symbolized in the four gospels.

Now look at chapter 6:2 as we see:

SEAL # 1 IS NOW OPENED:

WHITE HORSE—God's activity on earth. There is much dispute as to what this rider on the white horse represents. Some identify him as Jesus, because in Chapter 19 Jesus appears on a white horse, wearing a crown (a different kind of crown, however) and bringing to an end all the terrible series of judgments that have come upon the earth. But it is a mistake to identify these two because the context is entirely different. Here we are looking at the beginning of the judgments of God, and **in Chapter 19 we see the end of them.** The rider of Chapter 6 is summoned by one of the living creatures, but it would be unthinkable for a creature to summon the conquering Christ of Chapter 19. But it is

IS THE END NEAR???

significant that this rider on the white horse here **bears some resemblance to the appearance of Jesus on a great white horse in Chapter 19.** They both ride a white horse; **they both wear crowns;** and both are bent on conquest. It suggests that this rider is someone who is like Christ, **but is not Christ.**--CROWN: "stephanos" meaning the victors crown - and then there is "diadema" meaning kingly crown.

The Antichrist can never wear the diadema because it belongs only to the Son of God!

Many of you are already anticipating what I am going to say: This is doubtless the long predicted antichrist, whom Scripture speaks of in various places, who is yet to appear in the last days. The "Man of Sin" (2 Thessalonians 2:3 KJV) the Apostle Paul calls him, also "the Lawless One" (2 Thessalonians 2:8 NIV) who is yet to appear and offer himself as though he were God's Christ. Jesus himself said to the Jews of his day, **"I have come in my Father's name and you do not accept me, but if someone else comes in his own name, you will accept him,"** (John 5:43 (NIV)). This rider comes like Christ, but in his own name. He is given a bow, but no mention is made of arrows.

This appears to be a bloodless conquest he launches. When you ask, "What is this describing?"

I think it is clear that it suggests some kind of overpowering of the minds and wills of men, without

CHAPTER THREE

physical destruction. How is that done? The answer is -- by some form of deceit, by lying that misleads and deceives men and thus overcomes them without the shedding of blood.

If you will notice that this deceiver comes holding a bow but not arrows! Our Lord's weapon is a sword as we find in Revelation 19:15.

It is noteworthy that in Matthew 24, the first word Jesus speaks to his disciples is, "<u>Watch out that no one deceives you</u>," (Matthew 24:4). You will find references to the possibility of deception throughout that chapter.

We are bemused by delusions today. We are hardly aware of how much we are being deceived all the time.

- ▶▶ Turn on the television and fraudulent ideas, along with a mixture of truth, are immediately poured into your brain.

- ▶▶ Pick up a magazine or read a newspaper and you will find they make false claims that certain acquisitions will produce great blessing and liberty for you. But trying them will soon tell you that it is a lie. They do not work. We are constantly offered much of promise but which are totally unable to deliver.

- ▶▶ **Drugs deceive!** Millions of people, young and old, are being deceived by the flush of euphoria that a drug

IS THE END NEAR???

produces for a time. **Alcohol/wine, yes I said wine--- deceives!** Thousands have died because they have felt that drinking makes them feel sophisticated and mature. Many young people, especially, have been led into that trap. Perfume ads deceive! They offer outlandish, extravagant promises of rapture and romance that will follow if you merely douse yourself with something from a bottle. "HOG WASH!"

We are obviously living in a very deceitful age. What this rider on the white horse tells us, however, **is that the worst is yet to come**.

We are living amidst great deceit, it is true, **but it is not as bad as it is going to be. There is coming an even greater lie. Listen to the words the Apostle Paul said in 2 Thessalonians 2:9-12.**

Paul Herri—former Prime Minister of Belgium, the first Chairman of the General Assembly of the United Nations in 1945 said: "We do not want another committee, we want a man of sufficient stature to hold the allegiance of all people and lift us out of the economic morass in which we are sinking. Send us such a man and, be he God or the devil, we will receive him."

That makes it crystal clear, does it not? This first conquest by evil in the last days is set in motion when God takes off the reins and lets deceit have its way among men until it reaches a climax of delusion. (John 5:43). We will learn many more details of that as the book proceeds.

Now the **SECOND SEAL** is opened.

WATCH THIS NOW: "When the Lamb opened the second seal, I heard the second living creature say, "Come!" Then another horse

CHAPTER THREE

came out, a fiery red one. Its rider was given power to take peace from the earth and to make men slay each other. To him was given a large sword." (Revelation 6:3-4 NIV)

<u>SEAL # 2 - IS A RED HORSE</u>: s

>This rider is easy to recognize. **It is war, of course, but not war between great armies -- at least not at first. The word for slay is really the word "slaughter."**

>It is a reference to civil war or civil anarchy where mobs of people group together to attack and destroy other peoples whom they do not like. We are seeing a demonstration of this today in what is going on in AFGANISTAN, WITH ISIS AND IN AMERICA at this very time.

>We have had further examples of it in the gang wars raging in the streets of Los Angeles, Miami, New York City, Durham, NC, yes, even in Raleigh and other places. It is a murderous slaying of others by people **unrestrained by any control.**

>But that will lead to what is mentioned in the last sentence, **"to him was given a large sword."** In the days when John wrote they obviously did not have mega bombs, missiles, tanks, or any of the modern weapons of warfare. Such weapons of destruction had to be put in terms that people would understand in that day, so the major weapon of destruction then was a sword. But this is a "great" sword, a powerful weapon of destruction. It is with good reason that many commentators have seen this as a picture of the

IS THE END NEAR???

awesome power of a nuclear bomb, something that destroys enormous numbers of people.

If you read the 38th and 39th chapters of Ezekiel you will find a vivid description of such warfare, where armies come down out of the north into the Holy Land and are decimated by what appears to be radiation sickness. It is powerfully portrayed for us in those accounts.

SEAL # 3 - IS A BLACK HORSE - FAMINE!

Verses 5 and 6: *"When the Lamb opened the third seal, I heard the third living creature say, "Come!" I looked, and there before me was a black horse! Its rider was holding a pair of scales in his hand. Then I heard what sounded like a voice among the four living creatures, saying, "A quart of wheat for a day's wages, and three quarts of barley for a day's wages, and do not damage the oil and the wine" (Revelation 6:5-6 NIV)!*

Back in **WWII**, as a little boy of five, we were limited to certain items we could buy and with stamps, i.e. bread, sugar, gasoline, etc.

Most scholars take this to be a reference to widespread famine on the earth. They say that the scales symbolize food being weighed out carefully. It is in such short supply that it must be rationed. Even then no one can get very much because it takes a day's wages to earn a single quart of wheat or, because it is cheaper, three quarts of barley. This would

CHAPTER THREE

only be enough food for one person for a day. You would work all day long and all you would be able to earn at best would be enough for your own physical needs. There would be nothing for your family or for anyone else. But the luxuries, the oil and the wine, are left untouched.

But perhaps this is not referring to famine because in the next seal, as we will see, famine is specifically mentioned as part of that judgment. What else causes terrible shortages and creates high prices so that people cannot buy adequate amounts of food? It is inflation; economics out of control; panic in the marketplace! That in turn becomes an excuse for the rigid controls over buying and selling which we find in Chapter 13 when, under the reign of Antichrist, the whole world is subjected to enormously restrictive controls so that "no one can buy or sell without the mark of the beast," (Revelation 13:17) which we will look at in a future lesson.

That brings us to:

SEAL # 4 - IS A PALE HORSE (Verse 7) - DEATH!

When the Lamb opened the fourth seal, I heard the voice of the fourth living creature say, "Come!" I looked, and there before me was a pale horse!

The word actually is *chloros*, from which we get the word chlorine, a pale green horse, like chlorine in color. Its rider was named Death, and Hades was following close behind him.

IS THE END NEAR???

They were given power over a fourth of the earth to kill by sword, famine and plague, and by the wild beasts of the earth. (Revelation 6:7-8 NIV).

This rider is named "**Death**," and floating along behind, was a figure that is identified as "**Hades,**" **or Hell. Death takes the body** and **HELL takes the soul.** As someone has put it, "Death rides the horse, but HELL follows with the hearse." **There are four forms of death that are related to this attack.**

First, the sword, which here is not war but murder; individual assault upon one another. It is people taking the law into their own hands and murdering other people without regard to justice or law.

Second: With murder comes famine and widespread starvation. We are all familiar with the terrible pictures of famine areas, largely in Africa, and the swollen, distended bellies of little children with spindly legs as the flesh of their bodies disappears and they die a terrible death from starvation. Jesus spoke of such famines in Matthew 24.

Third: There would be on earth, he said, earthquakes, famines and plagues.

These plagues are endemic diseases. When civilization begins to crumble, the defenses of mankind against diseases are lost as well. Whole populations are decimated by such plagues. There may be a reference here to biological warfare, the willful

CHAPTER THREE

spreading of diseases among people so that they are wiped out in masses. It covers also the appearance of previously unknown diseases. We have a foreshadowing of these in the terrible plague of AIDS in our own day.

Fourth: The wild beasts of the earth multiply, and humans are subject to attack by these predators.

The account says that a "fourth of the earth" is given over to the four attacks. It is difficult to know whether that is a geographic or demographic division of earth. If it is geographic, then a fourth of the globe is decimated by these terrible plagues. **If it is demographic, it means a fourth of the population is taken.** There are approximately seven billion people on earth today and that would mean that one billion people, equivalent to the entire population of China, would be decimated by diseases. It is a picture of a desolated earth caused by man's hatred and barbarity.

These four seal-judgments are all references to forces that are already at work among us, but they will be carried to an unprecedented extreme in that day. Thus these four seals confirm God's announced method of making men face up to truth. **How does He make us stop hiding our heads and refusing to face reality?**

By allowing evil to have its full head! Romans 1 declares that he "delivers men over" (Romans 1:24, 1:26, 1:28) to their own passions, their own evil, and allows it unrestricted manifestation. God teaches us to face up to unpleasant truth by giving us what we demand.

IS THE END NEAR???

If men want to believe a lie - - then God will send the lie — **the lie of the Antichrist, the powerful delusion that Paul describes**.

If men seek to kill and destroy and refuse to see the evil of that, **then God gives them widespread anarchy, mob rule, and, ultimately, nuclear destruction.**

If men want more and more luxury and higher standards of living, they are given what goes along with it -- high inflation, which finally makes money worthless. If men demand power and control, what they are given is intrigue, murder, disease, and desolation in the earth. These cannot be stopped, because they are inescapable consequences of the evil of mankind.

<u>We have three more seals to look at in the series</u>, although only two of them appear in this chapter. In these two, no longer are natural forces allowed to have their head, but here is something quite different. We are shown supernatural activities; God working in the midst of the judgments of the four horsemen, both for good and evil. So we read of the opening of:

<u>SEAL # 5 - ARE SOULS UNDER THE ALTAR</u>:

Souls under the altar who had been slain because of the Word of God and the testimony they had maintained.

CHAPTER THREE

It marks the difference between time and eternity. The **altar mentioned** here has not appeared in this book before this. But it indicates, as will be confirmed by later references in this book, **that we are viewing the great temple in heaven, the temple which Moses saw when he was on Mt. Sinai.** He was shown a pattern which he was to copy in the tabernacle of old. He was ordered to copy it exactly as it was shown to him.

Thus the tabernacle contained a great brazen altar, and a laver in the outer court, a Holy Place with certain furniture, and a Holy of Holies, all reflecting the heavenly temple that Moses had seen.

We learn from other Scriptures that these symbolize the ultimate dwelling place of God which is man himself! Man is the dwelling place of God. When we come to the end of Revelation we will see that fulfilled. It is man who becomes the temple of God. These symbols are given to us as a tremendously significant explanation of the psychological makeup of our humanity -- body, soul and spirit -- just as the tabernacle consisted of an Outer Court, the Holy Place, and the Holy of Holies.

Let me quickly say this:

There is coming a day when everyone of these six seals will be opened one by one. And when all of that happens, there will be a colossal prayer meeting (Revelation 6:15-17).

IS THE END NEAR???

Isn't this amazing? They reject the Rock of Ages and pray to the rocks. You would think they would be praying to God. BUT instead they are praying to the forces of nature. The more sensible thing is not to be here when all this happens. If you want to go through the Great Tribulation, help yourself but I do not plan to be here. I am counting on meeting the Lord in the air on that glorious day!

Thank God there is a way out - - and that way is up - - It is **JESUS!!**

SEAL # 6 - A GREAT EARTHQUAKE - Revelation 6:12-14:

It is a vivid description of chaos in nature! The whole natural world goes on a rampage. Again, in Matthew 24 Jesus describes this same event, in verses 29-30:

"Immediately after the distress of those days" (He is talking about the great tribulation),

> "the sun will be darkened,
> and the moon will not give its light;
> the stars will fall from the sky,
> and the heavenly bodies will be shaken."

"At that time the sign of the Son of Man will appear in the sky, and all the nations of the earth will mourn. They will see the Son of Man coming on the clouds of the sky, with power and great glory" (Matthew 24:29-30 NIV).

These six seals have carried us almost to the very end of the whole seven-year period. We have been swiftly moving through this

CHAPTER THREE

dramatic period. After the great tribulation, nature will be upset by some cosmic phenomenon. Listen also to Luke, in Chapter 21:25-27.

It will be a time of terror and anguish throughout the earth. What will be the effect of this on the people? John now sees the final scene under the sixth seal.

<u>The Lamb</u>! "For the great day of their wrath has come, and who can stand?" (Revelation 6:15-17).

<u>Who can stand</u>? That is the question left hanging in the air. Of course, no one can stand. It is the end of civilization as we know it.

In that day, those who refuse to believe have reached a stage where they cannot believe. They do not repent and pray to the Lord for salvation. Rather, they feel a terrible fear and pray to the rocks to destroy them. They will manifest openly and publicly what they feel privately and secretly today. It is a strange phenomenon, but it is easily confirmed, that every unbeliever is convinced in his own heart that death is somehow an escape into oblivion! Somehow they think they can escape the terrible consequences of their evil by dying. That is why people commit suicide. They believe they are escaping their problems, that there will be no consequences beyond death. But the Word of God assures us this is not true: "It is appointed unto man once to die and after this the judgment," (Hebrews 9:27 KJV). **Why are we told these terrible truths?**

If we belong to the Lord now and are members of his body, the true church, **we will not be a part of this scene**. This is the great promise we have heard several times in Revelation up to this point. This whole terrible scene is specifically sent to the seven churches of Asia to read and understand. <u>**Why**</u>**? It is not only to make us earnest in our witness; it is also intended to show us where the forces and**

IS THE END NEAR???

movements which surround us at the moment are going to end up. We are told this so we can recognize evil while it still looks good, and thus be able to judge what to give ourselves to and what to reject. One verse in John's Gospel, Chapter 3, Verse 36, tells us the whole story:

> *"Whoever believes in the Son has eternal life, but whoever rejects the Son will not see life, for God's wrath remains on them"* **(John 3:36 NIV).**

I do not like preaching on these passages. I much prefer the wonderful views of the throne of God in heaven, with the angels singing around the throne the song of the redeemed. But if we are faithful to the Scriptures we must recognize that there is coming a day when the wrath of God must be poured out upon the unrighteousness of men and it is to that day we have come. Let us be sure that there is in none of us an evil heart of unbelief.

In the next chapter, he is going to open the missing seal, the seventh seal (Revelation 8), (aha!!).

CHAPTER THREE

THOUGHTS:

_____

_____

_____

_____

_____

_____

_____

ACTIONS:

_____

_____

_____

_____

_____

_____

CHAPTER FOUR

ANGELS

OF

DOOM

CHAPTER FOUR

In our studies in the book of Revelation we have been following the unrolling of the seven-sealed scroll which the Lamb of God won the right to open by His death upon the cross. The title of that scroll is "The Mystery of God," and when one reads Chapter 10 we will read that mystery -- exactly how God is going to bring about universal peace and joy to a sinful, angry, and murderous world -- is completed. God is doing that very thing with individuals even today. Many of you here have experienced the peace and joy which God gave you in the midst of the struggles and trials of your life. He does that by grace, by the offer of total forgiveness of sin. But to a world that rejects grace, God can only bring peace through judgment. That is what we are seeing in this book. Six of the seven seals have already been opened when we come to Chapter 8, and we have watched the waves of successive judgments roll across the earth. We learn from the prophet Daniel that these cover a seven-year period in the last days of this age. Under the seals, it is covered from one point of view, i.e., what happens when man is allowed to have his own way. All God does is to take away the restraints and let human evil

IS THE END NEAR???

find wider expression. It is limited slightly (to a fourth of the earth), but it finds far greater expression then than it does today. That brings us then to the seventh seal which is now opened to us in Chapter 8:

1. **THERE IS <u>SILENCE</u> IN HEAVEN: VERSE 1**

When he opened the seventh seal, <u>here is that missing seal</u> (aha!!).

Well, it must indeed have been an embittered and chauvinistic commentator who first suggested that this half an hour of silence proves there will be no women in heaven! **That, of course, is not the reason for it.** This word about silence reminds us of the prophet Habakkuk's cry, *"The Lord is in his Holy Temple; let all the earth keep silence before him!"* (Habakkuk 2:20 KJV).

This silence comes as a dramatic contrast to the shouting of praise and the playing of harps that has been going on in heaven up to this point. Millions of angels, hosts of redeemed humans, and other heavenly creatures have been crying out before the throne of God, and singing praises to him. **<u>But now suddenly everything ceases. When the seventh seal is opened there is total silence</u>**. It is a most dramatic pause. It reminds one of that moment of silence just before the last great "Hallelujah!" in the Hallelujah Chorus of Handel's Messiah. This is the silence of mystery, a silence of intense anticipation of what is about to happen. Authur Pink, in his commentary on Revelation says, *"It communicates in a dramatic way the full and awesome authority of God. Everything must wait for his kingly move."*

CHAPTER FOUR

Silence is a powerful thing. You can be about asleep in a service, but just let the preacher fall silent and you will snap to attention. The silence at the beginning of a wedding lets you know the time has come.

Silence can also be nerve shattering! Have you ever been listening to the radio or watching a TV program and suddenly there is silence? You immediately wonder what has happened at the station, don't you? Imagine you have asked your wife to marry you and she just sat in silence for thirty minutes.

Imagine you have been accused of a crime and the jury has come back with your verdict. You are standing before the judge waiting for him to read it to you, and for thirty minutes he just sits there in silence.

What we are seeing in this verse is the lull before the storm. The judgment of God is about to fall on the earth and Heaven has thirty minutes of silence before the judgments commence. *Habakkuk 2:20* says, *"But the LORD is in his holy temple: let all the earth keep silence before him."* Earth will not hear the Lord's voice, nor will they acknowledge Him at all. They rush on in their sins, living their vain lives, all the while ignoring the God of Heaven. The inhabitants of Heaven, on the other hand, understand what God is about to do and they fall silent in awe at His presence and His power.

That move begins, as this account tells us, with seven angels being given seven trumpets to sound. It is all part of the opening of the seventh seal. These are impressive angels indeed. We are told they are the angels "who stand before God." That calls to mind the story in Luke 1:19 of an angel sent to Joseph to tell him that

IS THE END NEAR???

Mary will be the mother of a child. The angel identifies himself as *"Gabriel, who stands in the presence of God,"* (Luke 1:19 NIV). These seven angels are probably archangels, and they are given an extremely important task in the sounding of these trumpets.

2. **THERE IS A <u>SERVICE</u> AT THE ALTER: VERSES 2-5**

Another angel, who had a golden censer, came and stood at the altar. He was given much incense to offer, with the prayers of all the saints, on the golden altar before the throne... Turn to Revelation 8:3-5 and read this passage.

Many of the expositors of Revelation identify this angel as Jesus himself. The reason is that in the Old Testament, while Israel is marching through the wilderness, they are led by a great angel called "the Angel of Yahweh," or, "the Angel of Jehovah." Most Bible scholars feel that it was an appearance of the pre-incarnate Christ, i.e., the Son of God himself, leading his people through the wilderness. Since Israel is in the forefront again in this book of Revelation, then it would make sense that the Angel of the Lord appears again in connection with that nation.

The New Testament also teaches us that Jesus is a great High Priest for his people. The book of Hebrews and a reference of Paul in Romans 8:34, tell us that Jesus is now a High Priest who *"makes intercession for the saints,"* (Hebrews 3:1, also, Romans 8:34 KJV). This is clearly what this angel-priest is doing here. He takes fire from the brazen altar, adds to it incense, along with the prayers of the saints, and offers them on the golden altar of incense before God. It is a wonderful portrayal that tells us much about the function of prayer.

CHAPTER FOUR

Do you ever feel that your prayers are not even heard, let alone answered? According to this, the prayers of saints, especially intercessory prayers (those we pray for others), are like fragrance in the nostrils of God. They delight him. He smells in them a remembrance of the character of Jesus, the One who gave himself for others. As these prayers are mingled with the incense provided by the great angel himself, (who may indeed be Christ), **they delight God.** But, more than that, they move God to action. If burning incense is symbolic of the prayers of saints who are imploring God to act -- then returning that fire to earth is a symbol of answered prayer. In other words, we have now come to the time when God will answer the prayers of his people. What is the result? We read, *"there came peals of thunder, rumblings, flashes of lightning and an earthquake."* You may remember that in chapter 4:5 these were the first sounds that John heard coming from the throne of God in the opening scene in heaven. He heard *"flashes of lightning, rumblings and peals of thunder,"* (Revelation 4:5b NIV). Here an earthquake is added to that as well. These sights and sounds mark the close of man's age, and the opening of God's kingdom upon earth.

In Chapter 11, at the last of the blowing of trumpets, we learn that when the seventh angel blows his trumpet the same sounds are heard and an angel proclaims that, *"the kingdoms of this world are become the kingdoms of our Lord, and of his Christ;"* (Revelation 11:15b). The scroll is then fully unrolled. These sounds come at the end of each of the series of seven: The seals, the trumpets, and the bowls of the wrath of God. Thus we learn here at the opening of this seventh seal, when the great Angel casts the fire of God back upon the earth, that the day has come when God answers fully the prayers of his people.

IS THE END NEAR???

There is one prayer that the people of God in all ages have been praying that has never yet been answered. It is clear from the Scriptures that this prayer was prayed by the saints of God from the dawn of the race. Adam probably prayed it when he left the Garden of Eden. Noah undoubtedly prayed it when he came out of the ark into a new world after the flood. Abraham surely prayed it as he looked for a City yet to come.

King David prayed it, and, when we come to the New Testament, all the apostles, including Paul, prayed this prayer. It is the prayer that Jesus taught his disciples to pray: *"Thy kingdom come, thy will be done on earth as it is in heaven,"* (Matthew 6:10, Luke 11:2 KJV). **That prayer has never yet been answered. We have not seen God's kingdom visibly on earth.** Invisibly it is present in the church and is seen in the rule of God over the affairs of men, but visibly the prayer has never been answered. But when we come to the end of these three series of judgments we will find that the prayers of men are at last to be fulfilled.

Let us come back to the seventh trumpet which probably begins what Jesus called in his Olivet Discourse, "the great tribulation." In Matthew 24 he says, *"For then there shall be great distress [tribulation], unequaled from the beginning of the world until now -- and never to be equaled again,"* (Matthew 24:21 NIV). It is the very acme of judgment.

1. THERE IS <u>SILENCE</u> IN HEAVEN

2. THERE IS A <u>SERVICE</u> IN HEAVEN

3. THERE IS <u>SUFFERING</u> ON THE EARTH

CHAPTER FOUR

In Revelation 8:6-13... we come to one of the most difficult sections of the book to interpret.

There is much debate as to whether these judgments are literal, reflecting some physical judgment upon the earth, or symbolic, a picture of something else much worse. My own view is that they are both! This is how God frequently works.

He pictures something invisible by means of a literal event. For instance, the sun is, of course, literal. It is a great shining star that warms our earth and keeps the whole solar system working. But it is at the same time symbolic, and is so used throughout Scripture. We refer to it in everyday life as a symbol of light, knowledge and truth.

Fire, too, is literal. You can burn yourself badly with fire -- but it is also symbolic of torment, torture and judgment.

The prophecy of Joel in the Old Testament opens with a vivid description of a plague of locusts that came upon the earth and ate up every green thing. Joel describes them in dramatic and accurate terms but his description soon becomes a description of the invasion of a great army from Babylon that will soon come into the land. Israel, throughout its history, used literal trumpets to indicate public warning of imminent action. So, through this series of seven trumpets we are hearing God's public announcement of severe judgment that is about to take place. These judgments are not something new in history. God has often acted in judgment upon men. Even today he is speaking to us of terrible moral failures by using actual literal events.

IS THE END NEAR???

       Take, for instance, the drug scourge which is such an enormous problem in our day, especially among our youth. Marijuana is now sold openly in many states and drugs destroy the mind, burn out the brain, and turn people into worse than beasts and animals. What is this scourge saying? Not only is it literal, but it is symbolizing the terrible danger of self-indulgence - the philosophy of self-fulfillment that is widely advocated in the media today. Self-indulgence, like cocaine or crack, lures us on by giving a sense of fulfillment and immediate pleasure. But the user is drawn on into a continuing orgy of self-indulgence until he finally finds himself living in the suffocating atmosphere of total self-centeredness. The drug scourge is the visual aid that God has given our generation to make us see what is happening to us at the root of our being. How blind we are to it! Jesus once rebuked the Pharisees of his day because they could interpret the signs of bad weather ahead, but they did not know how to understand the times.

       The AIDS epidemic is a very literal, frightening plague that has come upon us. It is consuming life after life in many countries today. We are now told that 50% of the women and 30% of the men in Uganda have AIDS. That country is facing almost total annihilation because of this fearful plague. We know how widespread it is here. It is literal, but what does it also symbolize? Just as AIDS robs people of their immunity against other infections, so, the Bible says, indulgence in sexual promiscuity robs us of any defense against the widespread theological and moral errors of our day. That is why people go for strange cults and strange teachings on every side today. **They are easy prey because their moral defenses have been torn down by sexual promiscuity. They have no moral immunity left.** Have you noticed the attention of this new danger called the **ZIKA** virus. In Paul's letter to the Ephesians he lists certain wrongful sexual activities, and says, *"Because of such things God's wrath comes on those who are disobedient,"* (Ephesians 5:6 NIV). The terrible scourge of abortion today, this awful murdering

CHAPTER FOUR

of unborn children, is obviously literal. The whole country is being torn apart over this issue at this present hour. But what is it saying, what is it picturing to us?

I think it pictures the moral sacrifice of our children, the loss of a whole generation of young people who are not being taught the truth about God. Watch them on the streets and in the ghettos of our great cities. Look into their listless, dull eyes. We are losing them. Like the ancient people of Israel, we are throwing our children into the vast burning jaw of the god Molech, deliberately sacrificing them to our self-centeredness. Abortion makes it horribly visible to those who wish to see.

Now let us look at these trumpets and see what they mean.

- ❖ **Angel #1 Sounds His Trumpet of <u>DEVASTATION</u>: Revelation 8:6-7.**

    This is very similar to the seventh plague that fell on Egypt during Moses' confrontation of Pharaoh, when hail and lightning came upon the whole land. Here, it is mingled with blood. This is not a new phenomenon. Scientists have recorded other times when red rain fell from the sky. They never could explain it fully, but it actually left great puddles of water that were as red as blood. Here is the same plague hitting the earth. It brings terrible destruction of the natural world. Notice that the plagues of the first four trumpets all fall on creation. **This is, in a sense, God's judgment upon a race that**

IS THE END NEAR???

destroys its environment. He is saying, in effect, "You want a destroyed world -- then you shall have it." This is fully in line with his methods of judgment.

But the destruction is not only literal, it is also symbolic. It is teaching something invisible to the eyes of men at that time. As we have already noted, the earth is used in Scripture as a picture of Israel, the intended model nation under God.

- Here is depicted a judgment upon Israel, both on its leaders (the trees), and upon its people (the grass).

- **Trees represent the pride of human greatness, flaunting the presence and the glory of God—** Daniel 4:20-22; Ezekiel 31:3-18.

- Grass is men generally, people generally—Isaiah 46:7. And the green grass, of course, would be the finest, the flower, the fruit of mankind—the best. When you go to war, whom do you destroy in war? Always the green grass, the flower and the fruit, the finest of the land. The prophet Jeremiah and other prophets of the Old Testament call attention to a time when God will judge his people Israel. Let me read such a prediction from the prophecy of Zephaniah. God says:

CHAPTER FOUR

"At that time I will search Jerusalem with lamps and punish those who are complacent, who are like wine left on its dregs, who think, 'The Lord will do nothing, either good or bad.' Their wealth will be plundered, their houses demolished. They will build houses but not live in them; they will plant vineyards but not drink the wine." (Zephaniah 1:12-13 NIV) Jeremiah calls this, *"the time of Jacob's trouble,"* (Jeremiah 30:7 KJV). That is the effect of the first trumpet. The second one follows:

❖ **Angel #2 Sounds His Trumpet of <u>DESTRUCTION</u>: Revelation 8:8-9.**

    The first trumpet judgment attacked the earth but this attacks the sea. A great blazing mountain is seen falling into the sea. Perhaps it is a volcanic eruption. It may be Mount Etna on the island of Sicily which volcanologists say is ready to blow its top, like Mt. St. Helens. Many scholars feel that the sea on which this judgment falls is the Mediterranean.

    Or perhaps it is a meteor falling out of space into the ocean. At any rate, the sea literally becomes blood red. Once again, this is not unknown. Every now and then the papers report what is called a "red tide" which appears in the sea and turns large areas of the ocean blood red. A tiny marine organism, red in color, multiplies at such an enormous rate that it makes the water look like blood. This plague destroys many of the living creatures in the sea; the ships are destroyed and the commerce of the ocean reduced by a third.

IS THE END NEAR???

But if it is literal, **it is also symbolic.** The symbol of a great mountain blazing with fire is that of a kingdom aflame with revolution. Jeremiah, for instance, describes Babylon as just such a mountain. He calls it a "blazing mountain" which is the destroyer of the earth (Jeremiah 51:24-26). It probably pictures, as we gather from other Scriptures, the rise of what is popularly called "the revived Roman Empire," the ten-kingdomed coalition of Western Europe and the Western allied nations under the Antichrist, which conquers the other nations of the earth. The sea is used frequently as a picture of the Gentile nations of earth.

Again, it is limited to one-third. Notice the repetition of this word **"the third"** all through the series of trumpet judgments. Under the seals the limitation was one-fourth of the earth. That is very meaningful. **Four is the number of human government, and under the seal judgments God is saying that he uses human government to limit the onslaught of the four terrible horsemen of chapter six.** Human government still retains some vestige of restraining power during those days. But here, even that is gone, and under the trumpet judgments only God himself restrains.

Three is the divine number and this is declaring that only God's mercy and God's grace limits these awful judgments to one-third of the earth.

Now we come to the third trumpet.

- ❖ **Angel #3 Sounds His Trumpet of <u>DEATH</u>: Revelation 8:10-11.**

    This great star which falls into the rivers and the fountains of earth, is very likely a comet which

CHAPTER FOUR

breaks up when it enters the atmosphere and scatters itself throughout the earth, falling into the rivers and springs and poisoning them with what is probably a form of radiation. We have had, perhaps, a kind of a fore gleam of this and a note of warning from God, in the terrible atomic accident that happened in Russia some years ago. It occurred at a city named Chernobyl -- and Chernobyl is the Russian word for Wormwood!

I read in the paper recently that a new comet has been spotted in the skies. It has been given the name "Austin," and will become in April the brightest object in the night sky. These comets flash into our solar system unexpectedly at times. No one knows where they come from or when they will arrive, and a new one has now been spotted. I am not saying it is the great star predicted here, but it indicates the suddenness by which such comets can appear.

At the same time that this physical event takes place, it will also symbolize something to happen in the invisible realm of man's internal life. Rivers, of course, symbolize masses of people moving in the same direction -- whole peoples who are caught up with one idea and moving like a river does in a predictable direction. **(WATCH THIS NOW!!!)**

The fountains denote the sources of moral or philosophical leadership, and a star is in Scripture the symbol of a prominent leader. It appears that some great personage, widely recognized as a leader, suddenly reverses his policy -- he "falls" in that sense. Many people are embittered by this and set against one another, resulting in widespread moral death. That is exactly what will be described later in Revelation under the rule of the Beast that comes from the earth, as we will see.

We will find a similar "star" in chapter nine when we hear the fifth and sixth trumpets of judgment. I will leave it at that for the moment.

- ❖ **Angel #4 Sounds His Trumpet of <u>DARKNESS</u>: Revelation 8:12.**

    Without preliminary comment I would like for you to read our Lord's words recorded in the 21st chapter of Luke, where Luke gives his account of the Sermon on the Mount of Olives. Look in verses 25-26 to see what Jesus says.

    That clearly is a reference to this same event under the fourth trumpet. But **not only is it <u>literal</u>** - the sun and the moon and the stars are, for one reason or another, darkened and fail to give their light for much of the time -- but it also symbolizes something. **Sun, moon and stars are used in various places in Scripture to typify earthly authorities.**

    - The highest, of course, is the king or president. He would be portrayed as the sun, and those under him would be as the moon and the stars. They symbolize a hierarchy of authority.

    - But what does this darkening mean, metaphorically? It pictures light withdrawn from the authorities of earth.

CHAPTER FOUR

- They are morally darkened and no longer display moral judgment. They are not governed by any sense of ethical restraint but become characterized by increasing deceit, treachery, merciless cruelty and a total lack of justice. Yet by the grace of God this darkening is still limited to one-third. Some restraint of evil is yet possible, but only by the sovereign grace of a sovereign God!

Verse 13 now warns us of an eagle who comes to declare that there is much worse yet to come. If you have a King James text, it reads "angel," but the better manuscripts use "eagle" here.

❖ **Angel #5 Sounds His Trumpet of DOOM: Revelation 8:13.**

> The fifth trumpet sounds, and there is an invasion from the bottomless pit. What you find here is that demons will be released upon the earth, watch this now: "from the bottomless pit." Who are these demons? Well, they will be especially vile, malicious and powerful; in fact they are so diabolical that God in His mercy prepared a special pit to which to lock them away until the appointed time!

It is interesting to note that these demons are not like demons who have roamed the earth since they fell from heaven. These dread to go to the pit to set the demons free! See Luke 8:31 and 2 Peter 2:4.

There are 11 things we need to learn about the demons from the abyss or the bottomless pit:

IS THE END NEAR???

1. They are **degenerate** spirits.

2. They are **darkening** spirits, Revelation 9:2.

3. They are **devouring** spirits, Revelation 9:3-4.

4. They are **debilitating** spirits, Revelation 9:5-6—in these verses we find they were not allowed to kill but to torment for 5 months.

5. They are **dauntless** spirits, Revelation 9:7.

6. They are **domineering** spirits, Revelation 9:7b—no human ingenuity will be able to stop them.

7. They are **deceptive** spirits, Revelation 9:7c—"like means faces" - a symbol of intelligence. The Antichrist will be craft and subtle. Adrian Rogers said, "I think the Antichrist will be so conniving that he will make you murder your mother and think that you are doing God a service."

8. They are **defiling** spirits, Revelation 9:8….meaning that womans hair is a symbol of seduction and defilement.

9. They are **defiant** spirits, Revelation 9:9….they cannot be stopped, outrun and no place to hide from them.

10. They are **durable** spirits, Revelation 9:10….five is a number of completeness and until their deed is done, they cannot be stopped.

11. They are **diabolical** spirits, Revelation 11-12.

CHAPTER FOUR

OK, NOW LETS LOOK AT:

THE SIXTH ANGEL THAT SOUNDS THE TRUMPET OF JUDGEMENT!

WE WILL TAKE THIS UP IN OUR NEXT CHAPTER!

IS THE END NEAR???

THOUGHTS:
_____
_____
_____
_____
_____
_____

ACTIONS:
_____
_____
_____
_____

CHAPTER FIVE

WHEN ALL HELL BREAKS LOOSE

IS THE END NEAR???

Oh, what a horrible vision and what a devastating visitation!

- **For we have come in the unfolding of this drama, we have come to the great final assault of Satan against God, and we have come to the final unfolding of the development of evil in this world.**

- **This ends the mystery of God's creative workmanship and God's elective purpose as He frames a new kingdom in which Christ shall reign and His subjects shall love and worship Him forever. These are the last and consummating days as God shall bring to pass in judgment His will in the earth.**

- In the unfolding of this final drama, we look at the seventh and the last seal (Revelation 8:1). And as

CHAPTER FIVE

that seal is broken, and the whole revelation is made of the counsel and purpose of God in the earth.

❖ The seventh seal becomes seven trumpets (Revelation 8:2) and those sounding trumpets are divided into two parts, into four and into three.

❖ The four first trumpets are sounded in the eighth chapter of the Revelation verses 2-13. The last three trumpets (Revelation 9:1-11:19) are so terrible and so horrible that they are set apart by an eagle flying over the meridian of this earth crying: ***"Woe, woe, woe, to the inhibiters of the earth by reason of the voices of the three trumpets which are yet to sound!"*** (Revelation 8:13).

❖ As tragic and as terrible as were the four trumpets that have already sounded, they are nothing to compare with the judgment and the visitation of these last three that God calls "the trumpets of woe" (Revelation 9:1-11:19).

In Revelation 9:1, the Greek word there, peptokota (fall), is in the perfect tense. Understand this please - They (the KJ translators) translate it here as though John saw that star fall. **No, John saw the star "fallen." It had already fallen—a past, perfect tense. Like the Lord Jesus said, "I saw Satan fall from heaven" (Luke 10:18). We do not know who this angel is. It could be Satan. In any event, when John saw him, he had already fallen. It refers to some great spiritual enthroned creation of God who was set as a luminary in God's heaven to uphold God's glory and God's moral government. And whoever this creature is - whether Satan or one of the archangels** who serve him - when John saw him, he saw him fallen from heaven unto the earth.

"And there was given to him the key of the bottomless pit" (Revelation 9:1). The Greek word there is abyss, and we have taken the Greek word bodily into our language - this fallen archangel, there was given to him the key of the abyss. Now, not only here, but in the Word of God, that abyss is looked upon as the darkness in which are imprisoned those fallen spirits who are reserved unto the Day of Judgment (Jude 1:6).

From This Sixth Trumpet We Learn:

First, that God can make one enemy of the church to be a scourge and plague to another.

Second, the Lord of hosts has vast armies at His command, to serve His own purposes.

Third, the most formidable powers are bounded by limits they cannot go beyond.

Fourth, when God's judgments are on the earth, He expects people to repent of their sin and learn righteousness.

Fifth, being unrepentant under divine judgment is a sin that will ruin sinners; for where **God judges He will overcome.**

Let me quickly say that idolatry is not a sin that will enslave <u>only the unsaved during the Tribulation</u>. It's a strong temptation for believers of every age, including our own. This truth convinces me

CHAPTER FIVE

that material things in our present generation are slowly calcifying our hearts to the spiritual things of God. Where that is happening, we also need to listen to God's warning and repent!

When we stand beside the Apostle John and through his visions witness the devastating impact of future judgments, we discover something utterly astounding about the depths of human depravity: No matter how extensive human suffering may be, **<u>the curse of spiritual depravity is overwhelming</u>**.

Look back at Revelation 9:21…..

One of the strange things about human nature—you don't change a man because of punishment. And you don't change a man because of incarceration or imprisonment. He may desist from evil because he is afraid, but his heart is still evil. He would do it if he could, or if he could get by with it.

You only change a man by the gospel of the grace of the Son of God. You only change a man in a new birth in a creation of a new love, a new devotion, a new commitment, a new vision, a new dream, a new life. That is why it is so everlastingly important for us not to build bigger jails. We are forced to do it sometimes, but that is no answer. We are forced to have juvenile homes for the delinquents, but that is no answer.

- ❖ The great answer for the changing of men lies in the power of the gospel of the grace of the Son of God.
- ❖ It lies in a new birth. It lies in a new home.
- ❖ It lies in a new commitment.
- ❖ It lies in a new dedication. It lies in a new love. It lies in a new faith.

IS THE END NEAR???

- ❖ It lies in the new man.
- ❖ And that's the reason we preach, and pray, and come and assemble ourselves together and join our souls, that in us maybe God will mediate the love and mercy that shall save our people from death.

CHAPTER FIVE

THOUGHTS:

_____

_____

_____

_____

_____

_____

_____

ACTIONS:

_____

_____

_____

_____

_____

CHAPTER SIX

IS THE END NEAR???

EARTH'S LAST TRIAL

CHAPTER SIX

Revelation Chapters 15-16

In our preaching through the Bible these many years, **54 to be exact**, I have been overwhelmed how this book has come alive in my life time in its prophecies.

Before I take you through chapters 15 and 16 I want to give you a quick overview of chapters 10-14, so that when you study this chapter, "Earth's Last Trial" you will have a better feeling for chapters 15 and 16.

Revelation 10 – The Bitter Sweet Book

Now, that little book in the hand of God sealed represented a forfeited inheritance. And the breaking of those seals represented the redemption of that inheritance and the casting out of the interloper, the usurper, that old dragon, Satan that took it away from God's man Adam (2 Corinthians 4:4), for whom God created these things (Genesis 1:26). Now, as each seal is open you have the story of how God cast out the usurper and the interloper and the intruder and how God redeems it back to man - - going to give it to us. We shall reign with our Lord, fellow heirs, kings and priests in the earth (2 Timothy 2:12; Revelation 1:6). And the story of that IS that each seal is broken. **This is the way God's is going to do it, until finally, the little book is opened** (Revelation 10:2), and you can see the whole broad outline of how God is going to redeem this lost creation back to man. Now, to me, that is the little book.

So this little book that is now open, the seals are all broken and it is a recounting - - **It is a revelation. It is an unveiling of how God will redeem.** How He is going to do it - - redeem this lost creation and give it back to these, to us for whom God made it (Genesis 1:26).

Revelation 12 - So in this passage, this Man-Child is born and is caught up to God in heaven (Revelation 12:5):

No reference to His life, no reference to His death, just that He is caught up to the throne of God in heaven. Then, this whole period of grace is omitted. And the whole story of church is omitted (Revelation 12:5-6). **WHY? Because He, God, is dealing here with Israel, with this woman who gave birth to the Messiah (Revelation 12:1-2). And Israel has no scriptural history in this day of grace.**

- ❖ The clock stopped for Israel when she rejected her Messiah and the 69 weeks was closed (Daniel 9:25-26). And in this present day, Israel is like any other people. <u>**They are lost without Jesus.**</u> **They have to repent.** They have to turn. They have to accept Christ as their Savior. They have to be born into the kingdom of God. They have to be regenerated, just like we are (John 3:3).

That lost Jew, that lost Gentile, that lost foreigner, that lost alien, that lost indigenous, that fellow-citizen, all of us are alike today. **But,**

CHAPTER SIX

God says, but there is coming a time when this age is finished and when the purpose of God for His church are done.

Revelation 13 - The Counterfeit Church:

We are speaking of the false prophet who looks like a lamb; he is soft and he is sweet and he is easy. And he counsels people and he speaks of their consciences and of their souls; **but he is the most dangerous monster of the two, for his heart and his leadership is of the Dragon. The Counterfeit Church** (AND IT IS ALIVE TODAY!!).

- ❖ It says what the people want to hear, saying it believes. It teaches what the world wants to hear taught.

- ❖ It enjoys what the world enjoys. I have a last characterization that is the truth of God: it offers an institutional salvation. The counterfeit church, counterfeit religion the false prophet; it offers an institutional salvation. That is, "You go with us and we will take you all to heaven by virtue of the fact that we are the church of God."

Revelation 14: **Trying** to find what God means by these marvelous revelations, to me is a very simple explanation.

<u>First of all</u>, the elders, they are twenty-four in number; **they represent the <u>resurrected</u>, <u>glorified saints of God</u>, twelve of the patriarchs, twelve of the apostles, AND there they are before God.**

It represents the old and the new, all of the saints of God – the old dispensation the old government, the old era, **saved by looking to the cross**; and the new dispensation, the new era, **<u>the age of grace</u>**

IS THE END NEAR???

in which we live, looking back to the cross. The elders represent all of the saved of God, twelve of the old, twelve of the new, twenty-four elders in the presence of the Lord (**Revelation 7:11; 11:16**).

OK- - - **NOW** we come to Chapters 15 & 16. . . . .

Chapters 15 and 16 go together. They are a part of the same vision – "**describing the seven last plagues**," in what is called in the last part of the eighth chapter of the Revelation, "**the last woe: the third of the three.** This section of 15 & 16 is also the judgment of the last trumpet; the seventh trumpet that is sounded in the last of chapter 11. In chapter 11, a temple of God was opened in heaven (Revelation 11:19), and that temple is seen now in chapters 15 & 16. In that eleventh chapter, the elders announced that the great day of the judgment of Almighty has come *"and the nations are angry, and the time is come that they which destroy the world should be destroyed:"* (Revelation 11:18). And that delineation is found in 15 and 16. In the last of the eleventh, the sounding of the seventh trumpet, the kingdom of this world is become the kingdoms of our Lord and of His Christ" (Revelation 11:15). And that ultimate and final preparation is found in this vision of the seven last plagues.

"And I saw another sign in heaven, great and marvellous, seven angels having the seven last plagues; for in them is filled up the wrath of God" (Revelation 15:1). There are three of these signs. In chapter 12, *"There appeared a great wonder in heaven, a woman clothed with the sun"* (Revelation 12:1). In the third verse, *"And there appeared another great wonder in heaven; and behold, a red dragon;"* then this third one, *"And I saw another sign in heaven; great and marvelous, the seven angels having the seven last plagues"* (Revelation 15:1). After the seals were the trumpets; after the trumpets were the bowls of wrath; and after the bowls of wrath, there is finished the judgment of God in the earth and the kingdom has come.

CHAPTER SIX

But before God describes those great and final and ultimate days of the visitation of His judgment, God gives us an incomparable vision here of the immortality, and the safety, and the salvation of His people who are standing by the fiery sea: **LET'S READ Revelation 15:2-3....**

What an incomparable vision! In the fourth chapter of the Revelation, **John saw before the great throne of the Almighty a crystal sea, a sea of glass, calm and beautiful.** Those elders that are there by the side of that quiet and beautiful and crystal sea <u>**are you and I**</u>, **God's sainted children of this day and of our age (Revelation 4:6-11).** But when he sees this sea there before the throne of God, and by its shores, standing the saints, he says this sea is a sea of glass "mingled with fire." **That is, these saints have come out of that great trial and tribulation.** *"And they sing the song of Moses the servant of God, and the song of the Lamb"* (Revelation 15:2-3). **You know, it is an unusual thing here, the first recorded song in the Word of God is the fifteenth chapter of Exodus - - the one we just sang, the one we just read – the song of Moses - - - - - - And the last recorded song in the Bible is the fifteenth chapter of Revelation, the song of Moses, the servant of God and the song of the Lamb.**

<u>**Watch this now:**</u> *"And to these were given the harps of God"* (Revelation 15:2). There are **<u>three groups in heaven</u>** to whom God places in their hands, to whom God gives the harps of heaven.

1. In the fifth chapter of the book of the Revelation – **to these who were raptured and taken up to glory (and that is we that have trusted Christ)** – they - we have harps from God (Revelation 5:8).

IS THE END NEAR???

2. In the fourteenth chapter of the Revelation, **the <u>one hundred forty-four thousand</u>** gathered to the Lamb on Mount Zion possessed the harps of God (Revelation 14:2).

Standing on the shores of the fiery sea, having the harps of God and singing the song of Moses and of the Lamb, a song of triumph and heavenly deliverance (**Revelation 15:2-3**) <u>are those having gone through the fire of the tribulation</u>. **FOLKS, WE HAD BETTER LEARN TO PLAY THE HARP!!!!!!**

Then he (John) sees the vision of the opening of the temple in heaven, "I beheld, and the temple of the tabernacle of the testimony in heaven was opened" (**Revelation 15:5**). **John saw into the very innermost shrine of deity itself, into the very heart of the sanctuary, into the center of the Holy of Holies.** And what he sees coming out of the very heart of the temple of God **is not the great Mediator, the High Priest, not ministering servants of mediation and grace and mercy**; but what he sees is this unusual and remarkable and astonishing **vision of seven angels** – priest angels – dressed like priests. And they are the seven angels of the seven last plagues (**Revelation 15:6**).

"And one of the four beast gave unto the seven angels seven golden," you have it translated here, "vials" (Revelation 15:7), as though it were bottles. Well, the Greek word is phi/ale, but the Greek word refers to **"shallow pans."** We call them "censers" in which the coals were placed from off the altar. And on top of the coals, **the incense was placed to burn unto God.**

These seven angels, by one of those cherubim – remember back there in the sixth chapter of Revelation **they are the instruments of judgment – one of them said to the first horseman, "Come," and the <u>white horse</u>,** and then the next one, "Come," and the <u>red horse</u>, then

CHAPTER SIX

the <u>black horse</u>, then the <u>pale horse</u> (Revelation 6:2-8). It is one of these cherubim that speaks and says to these seven angels, **"Take these seven censers."** And when they did so, and the seven angels received those seven censers, "The temple was filled with smoke from the glory and power of God; and no man was able to enter into the temple, until the seven plagues of the seven angels were fulfilled" (**Revelation 15:7-8**).

That is, the great and final interdiction of God has come. As God has set a boundary for the restless sea – thus far can the tides arise and no further, thus far can those waves beat and no more – so God has set a boundary to the evil of the nations of the earth. **And when that time comes, known to God, all mediation ceases.** <u>All intercession ceases</u>! The great and final unpardonable sin has been committed (**Mark 3:22-30**), and no man can enter that temple. It is shut and has become a temple of indignation and of wrath and of judgment until the seven plagues have been poured out into the earth.

<u>Then chapter sixteen is a description of those seven visitations</u>. *"And I heard a great voice out of the temple saying to those seven angels, Go your ways, and pour out the censers of the wrath of God upon the earth."* The holiness and the fragrance of the prayers and the intercession of God ascends up from His people - - **but to a people**: Who will not turn and who will not repent and who will not believe the Lord Jesus, **every one** of those censers, **every fragment** of its smoke, **every prayer of its intercession, every facet of its holiness becomes one of damnation and judgment! OH LISTEN FOLKS . . . . . .** What are these Seven Bowls?

<u>Bowl #1: Sores</u>. This bowl is a loathsome sore in verse 2 with a noxious odor, which falls upon those who have the mark of

IS THE END NEAR???

the Beast (666) and those who worship his image. (**Similar to Exodus 9:8-11**).

Bowl #2: The Bloody Sea. The oceans become like the "blood as of a dead man; and even living creatures in the sea died" in verse 3. In the trumpet judgment, the third part of the sea is turned to blood. God also turned water into blood to plague the Egyptians in the days of Moses (Ex. 7:15-25).

Bowl #3: The Bloody Rivers. God will judge the mass of murderers who flood the earth with men's blood by causing the rivers to become blood in verses 4-7.

Bowl #4: The Solar Furnace. The sun burns in verses 8-9. Solar energy will scorch mankind, who reject the Creator of all light, heat and energy which makes life on earth possible. Still they do not repent.

Bowl #5: Darkness. The seat (throne) of the Beast is darkened in verses 10-11. The Antichrist and all those who worship him as God, are thrown into total darkness. **They go mad, and gnaw their tongues for pain, yet still do not repent!**

Bowl #6: The Euphrates Dries Up. By drying up the great river, God creates a land route for the vast armies of the east as they march to their destruction at Armageddon in northern Israel in chapter 19:19-21.

Bowl #7: Babylon Destroyed. Because of its gross immorality, religious confusion and its souls belonging to Satan.

Dear folks, It is the judgment of God upon those who tread underfoot the grace of the Son of God, who despise the blood of the

CHAPTER SIX

covenant wherewith He was sanctified (Hebrews 10:29), who say "NO" to the wooings of the Holy Spirit and the calling of GOD! All of those things turn into condemnation and judgments.

That's one of the laws of God that is fearful to look upon. When God does a gracious thing for us, **He sends His Son for us and Christ dies for us,** and He raises up a God-called preacher to preach to man, and **that preacher opens the Book of God and pleads for men to come in repentance and in faith to Jesus**, and a wicked and a rejecting and a blaspheming unbeliever says, "No, I will not turn, I will not believe, I will not accept, **"then every gracious deed God has done turns into a fury and a judgment upon that Christ-rejecter."**

These are holy instrument censers that are used in the holy service of God in the temple. And now, spurned and blasphemed and rejected, the grace of God becomes fire, and indignation, and judgment, and fury. So they take these censers, each one of the seven angels, and they're poured out upon the earth.

Now, heretofore, when the seals were broken, there was deliberation, and when the trumpets were blown, there was deliberation. But as this thing moved toward its final climax, it moves furiously and fast, and immediately these things come to pass.

Now, in the time that remains I want to speak of just one of those.

Turn to Chapter 16:12-16. . . . . . .

One of the things, if I put it together, you will notice it. One of the things you will find in the word of God, that wherever the thing starts, and whatever the section may be discussing, it always ends in that great final battle of the Lord God Almighty called the

IS THE END NEAR???

battle of Armageddon. Back there, this thing went on and went on and continued and it continued, and in the fourteenth chapter of the Revelation, it ended in that great battle of the day of the Lord. And here in the fifteenth and the sixteenth chapters, it does the same thing again. It ends in the great battle of the day of the Lord; and in the next section, 17, 18, and 19, the nineteenth chapter ends in that same great battle of the day of the Lord. **God's Book says that time, and history, and government, and preparation inevitably moves toward a great and final and indescribable conflict in this earth.**

Now the strange thing about it, as you read the Bible, is that all of these armies and all of these leaders are gathered in Palestine. They are all there – how could you get the armies of the earth there? For example, the sixth seal says one of those armies numbered two hundred million men (**Revelation 9:16**). It is a fantastic, astronomical number! **There in the battle of Armageddon are the armies of the earth, and the leaders of the earth, and the chiefs of staff of the earth. How is it they are all there?** Well, no strategy on the part and no wisdom on the part of government and armies and people would ever do a thing like that. That is the reason he explains – (**Revelation 16:13-14, 16**).

You have an illustration of that same thing in the story of Ahab in I Kings the twenty-second chapter. **Do you remember the story of Ahab in I Kings 22:34-38? That is what is going to happen, God says in this last great battle. The spirit of evil, out of the dragon, out of that trinity of evil, is going to persuade these armies and these leaders to gather in Palestine, and there that great battle is going to be fought.**

How come these vast armies are in Palestine? How come these great leaders of the world are in Palestine, where this awful thing

CHAPTER SIX

can happen, blood two hundred miles long, flowing, and a river of destruction?

"I saw three unclean spirits, and they went forth unto the kings of the whole world to gather them together to the battle of the great day of God Almighty" (**Revelation 16:13, 14**). For you see – and right here is a little sentence, and you wonder, well, **why is that there?** Right in the middle of that, for they are the spirits of evil going forth to persuade. "Behold, I come as a thief" (**Revelation 16:15**). **Why is that there?**

Why, it is very simple. If a man will not hear the voice of God, he lays his heart open and his life open to listen to the voice of destruction and evil and judgment and damnation! When the kings of the earth and the people of the earth and the armies of the earth won't listen to God, then, **of course, they lay themselves and their people open to listening to the persuasive voice of the spirits of darkness and evil. And that is why the little verse: "Behold, I come as a thief. Blessed is he that is ready."** Oh, listen to the voice of God!

This brings us to the Battle of Armageddon . . . . I will just give you a small glimpse of it (Hebrew name: Mount Megiddon) . . . it sits quietly at the break of the north-south chain of the Anti-Lebanon mountains and is beside the great north seaport of Haifa, which can allow munition and troopships by the hundreds to dock and unload.

1. It is a real geographical site in <u>**northern**</u> Israel.

2. God named this as the scene of the <u>**final**</u> battle of this age.

3. The armies that gather at Armageddon will come at the call of <u>**Satan**</u> (verses 13-14).

IS THE END NEAR???

4. The armies of the kings of the **east** will come – the 200 million.

5. The aim is to destroy Israel once and for all (Zechariah 12:2-3).

6. God will appear and rescue **Israel** (Revelation 14:20) and Israel will at last look in faith at her long-awaited Messiah (Zechariah 12:10-11).

7. At this time Christ will come with His **church** (Revelation 19:14).

8. Christ will subdue and destroy the forces of **evil** (the number eight is the number of Jew's New Beginnings).

And then this chapter closes – and I hate to close. Then the chapter closes: *"And men blasphemed for the plague was great"* (Revelation 16:21). Wouldn't you think they would turn? O God, the falling government! O God, the oppression! O God, the darkness! O God, the judgment! Save us! Isn't it remarkable?

They just blasphemed God the more. Isn't that what you see in the world today? **Oppressed and in chains and in slavery, turn to God? Call on the Lord? NO! NO!**

NO sign of revival. No sign of appeal. No sign of repentance. No sign of turning. It is the spirit of depravity in the world.

That is why the preaching of the gospel!!!!

That is why we are trying to get you to see through these writings, and why this invitation for you and for our people are so important. **PLEASE PRAY: God, be good to us and merciful to us and save us.**

CHAPTER SIX

<u>I AM PLEADING</u> - - - PRAY FOR GOD TO BRING REVIVAL IN AMERICA, IN OUR CHURCHES AND IN OUR OWN PERSONAL LIVES. WANT YOU JOIN ME.

PLACE THIS IN YOUR PRAYER JOURNAL SO YOU WILL NOT FORGET TO DO SO.

IS THE END NEAR???

THOUGHTS:
_____
_____
_____
_____
_____
_____

ACTIONS:
_____
_____
_____
_____
_____
_____

CHAPTER SEVEN

ONE THOUSAND YEARS OF PEACE

IS THE END NEAR???

Revelation 20:1-6

The subject for us to look at now is about the triumphant and glorious kingdom, the millennial age of our Lord and the **ONE THOUSAND YEARS OF PEACE!!!**

These messages have come and gone so fast that I wish I had more nights to preach on this subject. The fullness of the riches of the revelation of God in what He has prepared for His children is <u>immeasurable</u>. It is **<u>unfathomable</u>**. It is **WONDERFUL and we have just touched the hem of the garment in the few messages**.

NOW, we are going to look at this glorious day that God has promised for His Son **and for us who know Jesus Christ as our Saviour on this earth**.

As long as the human race has lived, just so long has **<u>there been a dream of a golden age</u>**. Time and again will you find it here in the Word of God, prophet after prophet, apostle after apostle, book after book, will you find it recorded here in God's Holy

CHAPTER SEVEN

Word. There is more said in the prophetic Scriptures regarding this millennial age than of any other one thing in the prophecies themselves. CAN YOU JUST IMAGINE WHAT THE GARDEN OF EDEN WAS LIKE????

CAN YOU JUST IMAGINE A TIME when there will be **NO MORE POVERTY** and **EVERY PERSON** will have all that his heart desires? No more prisons, no hospitals, no mental institutions, no need for any armies, the implements of war will be relics of the past.

Israel will be restored to her land and Jerusalem will be the world's capital. Now just watch this: no gambling dens and no houses of prostitution.

JUST THINK OF THIS: The bloom of youth will be on everyone's cheek. **The resurrected saints will rule and reign with the Lord Jesus Christ!!**

Theologians are divided on whether there will be a thousand-year reign or Golden Age. There are basically **three interpretations about the millennium**: amillennialism, postmillennialism, and premillennialism.

- ❖ The **amillennialist** believes there will not be a literal millennium. If you put the alpha prefix in front of a word, it simply negates the meaning of the word. For instance, the word amuse means "not to think." **If you want to think**, you go to a museum. The amillennialist take all the promises given by God to Israel in the Old Testament and apply them to the New Testament church.

IS THE END NEAR???

- ❖ Next is the <u>**postmillennialist**</u> view. <u>**The prefix post means "after." They believe that Jesus is coming after the thousand years of peace on earth**</u>.

    There are not many postmillennialists around today, because their theory that the world is getting better and better is rapidly being disproved by the reality that our world is going deeper and deeper into sin, of which the Word of God teaches.

- ❖ **NOW, AS A CHURCH,** we believe in the "<u>**premillennialist view**</u>" and that is this: **We believe that Jesus must come before the church can enjoy a thousand years of peace on earth. We believe that Jesus will come in power and great glory and He will rule and reign from Jerusalem. We also believe that God will give His nation Israel a second chance to repent and rise to political greatness.**

In this day and age, the premillennialist's goal is to prepare people for the second coming of Jesus Christ by preaching His glorious saving grace.

This is the time called "the Golden Age (or the millennium of Christ's reign on earth.) The English word "millennium" comes from two Latin words: **mille which is a "thousand." and annum which is a "year."** So millen-annum, "millennium" is a thousand year period. It is a time period just like an hour is a time period, a year is a time period, a century is a time period; so a "millennium" is a time period. But so

CHAPTER SEVEN

preeminent and so celestially glorious is this prophesied millennium that we have come to refer to it as the millennium. Look at the references to this 1,000 year reign: **Revelation 20:2-7**.

It begins after Satan is bound, after the great battle of Armageddon (**Revelation 19:11-21, Revelation 20:1-3**) and it ends after a thousand years, when Satan is loosed for a little season (**Revelation 20:7-10**). It is a new age, it is a new order. **And there are many things concerning it that we cannot conceive, we cannot understand, and there's no need to try.**

I cannot conceive of a world—we cannot conceive of a world without sin, where Satan is bound, where righteousness reigns; and many of the scholars believe, in which there is no death.

Now having giving you a small introduction, let me give you five basic things about the **"THOUSAND YEARS OF PEACE or THE GOLDEN AGE" that will usher in the rule and reign of Jesus Christ on earth.**

1. **THE FORCEFUL Restraint of Satan** - Revelation 20:1-3

    That brings us to the question: "**where is Satan today?**" I Peter 5:8 tells us he is roaming the earth to find people that he can destroy and deceive. By the way, you and I need to (1) **RESPECT** him, he is dangerous—don't joke about him. How are you living tonight knowing that he is on the loose? (2) **RECOGNIZE** him for he is the great pretender and always be on your guard....(3) **RESIST** him. Take your stand on God's Word. Remember James 4:7 says, "*resist the devil and he will flee from you.*"

IS THE END NEAR???

Now according to this passage in chapter 20, he will be chained and cast into prison; actually God's Word calls this prison a bottomless pit and that will not be Satan's final destination; it will be a holding tank until he is finally cast into the lake of fire. If you will remember that back in chapter 4 we saw where Satan was the original holder of that key and in chapter 9 we learned that he will open the bottomless pit and loose the demon horde upon the earth.

I like how God used Isaiah to give us a brief overview of Satan's biography and prophecy of his end in the bottomless pit: Isaiah 14:12-17. Adrian Rogers said of this verse: ***"they will have to squint to see him."***

Yes, he may be loose on the earth today, **but one day we will see him in forceful restraint.**

2. <u>**THE FUTURE Reign of the Savior**</u> - Revelation 20:4-6

After the great Tribulation and the battle of Armageddon, Jesus Christ will literally reign on earth for a thousand years and the saints will reign and rule with Him. How do we know this? Because Jesus taught us to pray: "<u>*Thy kingdom come. Thy will be done on earth as it is in Heaven*</u>" (Matthew 6:10). **Let me ask you this question! "Has His will been done on earth as it is in Heaven?" NO!! Will it be? YES--- WHEN HE RETURNS FOR HIS millennium reign. Let's look at the <u>changes</u> that will take place:**

A. The **<u>human</u>** kingdoms will change (Isaiah 2:2-4).
B. The **<u>animal</u>** kingdom will change (Isaiah 11:6-9).

CHAPTER SEVEN

C. The **plant** and **mineral** kingdoms will change (Isaiah 35:1).

3. **THE FIRST Resurrection**

Revelation chapter 20 tells us that there will be a first resurrection.

Pay close attention now; this is not a general resurrection, as some believe. *"Blessed and holy are those who have part in the first resurrection."*

What is the first resurrection? Well the Bible gives us the analogy that **the first resurrection is like a harvest, which has <u>four general aspects</u>**.

❖ The **firstfruits**. In the Old Testament, when the harvest ripened the priest went into the field and gathered a sheath of first-ripened grain. Then he took that sheath into the temple and waved it before the Lord. It was called a wave offering. He would say something like: *"Thank you, Lord, for this sheath of wheat, for we believe it is a promise of the harvest to come."*

Well, in the New Testament, **<u>Christ is called the firstfruits</u>**. Turn to **I Corinthians 15:20-23. Watch this now: When Jesus arose from the grave, <u>He became the firstfruits</u>. <u>His resurrection demonstrated that a harvest would come</u>.** As a matter of fact, Matthew tells us that when Jesus breathed His last words on the cross and the veil of the temple was torn from top to bottom, *"the* *tombs also were opened and many bodies of the saints who had gone to their rest were raised and they came out of the tombs after His resurrection, entered the holy city, and appeared to many"* (Matthew 27:52-53). So then, these saints were considered part of the firstfruits in the first resurrection.

❖ The **general** harvest. When Christ comes again, He will rapture the church. This is considered the general ingathering of the harvest (I Thessalonians 4:16-17).

❖ The **gleanings**. The third phase will be the resurrection of the tribulation saints----many of whom will be "beheaded" for Christ. These are the ones referred to in Revelation 20:4. **WOW!!**

❖ The **Rulers** with Christ. Other than the Lord Jesus, who will rule during the millennium? Not the angels! There is a world to come, but the angels are not in charge of it (Hebrews 2:5 and I Corinthians 6:2-3).

This passage not only has application in the reign and rule of Christ and His saints during this glorious age, but it also has application for us today. If the church will have the future responsibility of judging angels, doesn't it make sense that we can resolve problems in the church today?

Romans 16:20 Promises: *"The God of peace shall bruise (crush) Satan under your feet."* Oh how great it will be in that day when the criminal is in prison

CHAPTER SEVEN

and Israel is back in her land, and the bride is with the bridegroom and King Jesus in on **HIS THRONE?** **Yes, dear Christian, that will be the Golden Day !!!!!**

4. <u>THE FINAL Rebellion of Sinners</u>

Just when we think we have it made with the Devil, bound in the bottomless pit, **<u>he comes out again</u>**. But it is not a jailbreak.

He is released! God, who is always sovereign, <u>allows</u> <u>Satan</u> to have one final fling. Why? This is God's final test of mankind. Turn to Revelation 20:7-9.

Maybe you are thinking at this point, "Won't everyone be saved during the millennium?" **NO!** During the 1000 years of glory, Jesus will rule the nations with a rod of iron, but something will happen. **Hearts will turn, but it will not be because Satan will lead a rebellious uprising. But latent in the human heart, men will covet sin that has not been washed by the precious blood of the Lord.**

This may shock some of you, but people will have children during the millennium and when they have children, many of these children will not repent and believe upon Jesus Christ as their Savior and Lord!! God has millions of children, but He has no grandchildren. Just because one generation is Christian doesn't mean the next generation will be. By the end of the thousand years, the world will be filled with numerous generations of their descendants, who will still have bodies of mortal flesh and, more importantly, will still struggle with sin

and temptation as we do. Those subjects of the kingdom will not be like the resurrected, who will be immortal, glorified and neither marrying nor giving in marriage (Matthew 22:30).

Yes, during the 1,000 year reign the physical world will be made like Eden, harmonious and peaceful (Isaiah 65:20-25). **Yes, the corrupt system of human government underwritten by Satan and his demonic powers will be replaced by Christ and His saints** (Daniel 7:21-22)

However, the human population <u>**will still have a sinful nature**</u>—after the likeness of fallen Adam rather than perfected and glorified after the likeness of Christ.

Satan's brief release and humanity's futile rebellion prove two things: the total incorrigibility of Satan and the total depravity of humanity. As inconceivable as it may seem, **not all children born during the Millennium will be loving and loyal subjects of Christ.** Though Christ's reign will turn the world right side up, **many hearts will remain upside down.** Outwardly they may conform, but inwardly they will harbor bitter feelings that will be ripe for the harvest when Satan arrives with a message to match their hidden malice. Make no mistake, the human heart remains deceitful and desperately wicked!!!

Now, when **God** lets Satan out of the bottomless pit, He, God, is demonstrating to the world <u>**two great principles**</u>.

<u>**Man's Solution is Not the Final Answer**</u>.

- ❖ <u>**Punishment is not the answer**</u>. When God releases Satan, he would have been in prison for 1,000 years doing hard time.

CHAPTER SEVEN

Now God being an all knowing God, knows that punishment is not the answer---prisons are not the answer---they are necessary—but they are not the final answer!

❖ **Changing the environment is not the answer**. Don't forget that it was in **The Garden of Eden** when man got into trouble and what greater place to have lived than there?????

I don't care if we make the environment as good as we can, there will always be sin in the human heart!!

Listen: the criminologist and his prisons are not the answer. The sociologist and his programs are not the answer. The educator and his philosophies will not solve the problem of sin.

The only hope for man is **JESUS CHRIST!!!!**
John 14:6 - "I am the way.... except through Me."

5. THE FIXED RESOLUTION OF SIN

Have you ever thought that we could ever say goodbye to sin? Well I have good news for you! Turn to **Revelation 20:9-10**.

The Word of God clearly declares that Christ's Kingdom will last forever (Revelation 11:15). Listen closely now: The conditions of peace and righteousness established by Christ will last forever.

IS THE END NEAR???

The Bible is clear about that. Satan and his false messiah will never again have power over the earth. **Christ and His saints will never be dethroned. The earth will never again be cursed.**

Let me just quickly say this: *"If the kingdom of Christ and His saints will last "forever and ever,"* why does Revelation 20 refer to the reign of Christ lasting only one thousand years?

Well, in truth, the millennial reign is actually the first thousand years of Christ's eternal reign. The condition of peace and righteousness established by Christ will last forever.

The Bible is very clear about that. Satan and his false messiah will never regain power over the earth. Christ and His saints will never be dethroned. The earth will never again be cursed. Yet in another sense, **this specific phase of Christ's rule** will come to an end after a thousand years, and the final phase of His reign will begin.

Folks let me encourage you that God lets Satan loose only for a **season.**

THEN, God will end Satan's reign of terror by ultimately casting him and his demonic rebels into an eternal lake of fire (Matthew 25:41). Friend why follow a looser? Turn to I Corinthiana 15:24-25. Let me give you four truths from this passage:

❖ It provides for us **encouragement**. The gospel has not failed. We are not postmillennialists who are trying to make the world better so Jesus can come.

CHAPTER SEVEN

- ❖ This truth brings **anticipation**. Jesus can come at any moment! Turn to Matthew 24:44. Over and over in the Bible it tells us about the imminent return of the Lord Jesus Christ.

- ❖ This truth puts our focus on **evangelism**. Is there a passion in your heart to bring people to Jesus Christ so they might be saved? If not, then ask God to give you one!!

- ❖ This truth challenges us to do an **examination** of our lives. Are you truly born again (Ephesians 2:8-9). Oh what a wonderful gift!!!!!

Well we close now and Revelation chapter 20 tells us that there will be a forceful restraint of Satan, a future reign of the Savior, a final rebellion of sinners, and a fixed resolution of sin.

ARE YOU READY FOR THE FUTURE??????

IS THE END NEAR???

THOUGHTS:
_____
_____
_____
_____
_____

ACTIONS:
_____
_____
_____
_____
_____

CHAPTER EIGHT

THE CITY

OF

GLORY

IS THE END NEAR???

Revelation 21:9 - 22:7

*W*ell, I have got good news! That is the way I would like to start this last chapter from the book of the Revelation. It is indeed good news!

- ❖ The judgments are past, the terrible plagues upon the earth are ended.

- ❖ We begin with a view of heaven coming down to earth; a time when the prayers of God's people for centuries, **"Your will be done on earth as it is in heaven," will be answered.**

Chapters 21 and 22 contain almost all the Bible records concerning the eternal state. Most of the prophetic passages of the Old Testament that picture a time of great blessing on earth refer to the thousand-year reign of our Lord which precedes this last great event. Very little is said in the Old Testament about heaven. But here it is in these chapters. <u>Following the Great White Throne</u>

CHAPTER EIGHT

Judgment, recorded in Chapter 20, by the way, if you are a child of God, i.e. "born again"………. you will not be there or **will you care what is going on at that judgment!!!**

Now, for our <u>final chapter</u>, which is on the Holy, Heavenly City of God. Revelation 21:9 through Revelation 22:7. Now, this will be an exposition of this passage.

In this vision, John sees the Holy City, **<u>the New Jerusalem</u>**, and he describes it first from the outside as he saw it descend out of heaven. Then he describes the inside as though he entered within the gates of the city. Now, this is the description of the outside from verses 9-11—let's read this…………

I think it is a diamond; all of these stones that are named here in the Bible; they have just taken the Greek word and put it in the English language. We just suppose that they are this and this is this. But I think that the *iaspis* **stone**—when you get in English, it is pronounced **"jasper"—I think it is a diamond**. Every description I find of it in the Revelation is like that. This holy city, having the glory of God, with a light likened unto a stone most precious, "even like a jasper stone, clear as crystal." What you call jasper is not clear as crystal, **but a diamond is**, and it has the glory of the fire of God in its heart.

OK, now look at verses 12-21……..Now, each one of these twelve jewels are going to be named. Each one of them is a Greek name. They have just taken the Greek word and spelled it out in the alphabet and pronunciation of our English language.

And now we're going inside the city. He's described it as it descended from God out of heaven.

IS THE END NEAR???

And he looked at it, saw it measured, and described its glory and light and beauty and wonder. Now he comes to the gate and enters into the city, and he describes what's inside. Let's read verses 22-27…..

Alright let's read Revelation 22:1-5………..And the vision ends. Then we have an epilogue, a benediction, an affirmation, an authentication, **and God's Holy Word is closed**.

The beautiful, heavenly, and Holy City of God—oh, what a delightful, glad, glorious prospect! And what a precious revelation this vision here John saw when he looked upon the city descending out of heaven from God, *"And there came unto me one of the angels… and talked with me, saying, Come hither, come here, I will show thee the bride, the Lamb's wife"* (Revelation 21:9).

And when he looked upon her, he saw a city, great and holy, a new Jerusalem in contrast to the old, descending out of heaven from God. So it is a city, real and actual, and it is called <u>the bride, the Lamb's wife</u> because of those who inhabit it, its occupants, its dwellers. The Lamb's wife, the bride, living in a great and a beautiful and a golden city, whose builder and maker is God.

That bride is the church, the bride of Christ, the Lamb's wife. But in the city is not only the saved in the fellowship of Christ's church, but in that city are her attendants and her friends, and those who were invited to the marriage supper of the Lamb.

In Revelation 19:7-9 it says: *"Be glad and rejoice: for the marriage of the Lamb is come, and His wife hath made herself ready."* That is the church, the bride of the blessed Lord Jesus.

But not only is she there—**<u>the church taken out of the side of our Lord</u>**, born out of the suffering and the crimson of our Savior—not

CHAPTER EIGHT

only is she there, but in the verse that follows: "And blessed are they who are called unto the marriage supper of the Lamb."

Not only is there a wedding, when the bride of Christ is presented to Jesus, but there is also a marriage supper! And to that marriage supper there is a special benediction for the guests who are invited. Some of those friends of the Bridegroom are men like John the Baptist, who never lived to be a part of His church; who are in no sense a part of the bride of Christ. They died in the old dispensation. But lest someone think they might be less blessed, there is a special beatitude for them: *"Blessed are they also"*—beside the bride who has been married to the Lamb—*"blessed are they also who are called to the wedding supper, the marriage supper of the Lamb"* (Revelation 19:7, 9).

So in that beautiful city, there is not only the bride of Christ, but there are her attendants and her friends. And there are these who are called to the marriage feast, all of the saints of the old dispensation and the old covenant. Even our Lord said, *"There shall be many from the east and the west, who shall sit down in the kingdom of heaven with Abraham, and Isaac, and Jacob"* (Matthew 8:11).

So when we come to live in that beautiful city of God, we shall see not only these who have been saved in this age and dispensation, the bride of the Lamb, but we shall see also those who have been converted and saved, from the days of Abel to the last martyr slain by the Antichrist. All of God's redeemed saints shall live in that beautiful and holy city. I would think that also from the names that are written on it, *"…had a wall, great and high, and twelve gates, and the names of the twelve tribes of Israel on those gates"* (Revelation 21:12). As Jesus said, *"Salvation is of the Jews"* (John 4:22). God gave to them the oracles of the Lord. And their names—those twelve tribes representing all of the saved of the old covenant—their names are on the twelve gates of the beautiful and heavenly city.

"And the walls of the city had twelve foundations, and in them the names of the twelve apostles of the Lamb" (Revelation 21:14). And in that city are those who are saved in this day and in this age and in this dispensation. That's the reason I think the elders so frequently referred to in the Apocalypse are numbered twenty-four—twenty-four elders, twice twelve. They represent the twelve patriarchs of the old covenant; they represent the twelve apostles of the new covenant. And the twenty-four elders represent all of God's redeemed of all of the ages, carried into heaven, resurrected from the dead or raptured and changed at the Lord's coming, and all of them living in the beautiful and heavenly city of God (Revelation 4:4; 19:4-5).

As I describe the new heaven and the new earth (Revelation 21:1) that God's going to **remake it, regenerate it, redeem it, refurbish it, and re-establish it in holiness and glory** as He did in the beginning, before sin cursed and destroyed it—now wait a moment, when I describe the new heaven and the new earth and speak of our dwelling here in this earth, someone might think, *"Well, I thought we were going to heaven when we die. I did not know we were going to stay down here in this earth."*

Well, we do go to heaven when we die. Our home is in heaven. **Our house, our mansion, our dwelling place, our abiding place is in heaven.** It is in this beautiful city, this heavenly, holy, New Jerusalem. **But in God's day and in God's time, the purpose of God's redemption is**

CHAPTER EIGHT

to make a new heaven and a new earth that His new city might come down and dwell and be placed on this very and same terrestrial globe.

I think that is the meaning of these revelations: a new heaven above us, and a new earth beneath us, and a new heavenly city, our home, coming down out of heaven ***"from God"*** *(*Revelation 21:2). Those little Greek prepositions mean so much. He saw that city, coming *"from God,"* apo tou theou, *"from God,"* but ek tou ouranou, *"out of heaven."* It's not coming ***"from"*** heaven as though it might be nearby or close, but it is coming *"out of"* heaven. When we go to heaven, our heavenly home is that beautiful city. And it comes out of heaven from God.

That's where we go when we die, and we shall come from heaven. That's where the marriage supper of the Lamb is going to be, in heaven (Revelation 19:6-9). That's where the wedding feast is going to be, is in heaven. And in God's providence, at the end of these great and climactic and heavenly days, out of heaven shall descend this incomparable and beautiful city!

Then John describes it as he saw it. And he measures it and tells us what it looks like. He said it is a perfect cube: it's foursquare (Revelation 21:16). And then he described its size, and speaks of its color and then of its symmetry and proportion, its sides.

Oh, how tremendous and how great God is preparing that, our Lord Jesus is preparing that for us now! When our Savior went away, He went away to do two things: one, to pray for us, to intercede for us. Our great holy High Priest who entered into the veil, there to make intercession for us: ***"Wherefore He is able also to save them to the uttermost that come unto God by Him, seeing He ever liveth*** *to make intercession for them"* (Hebrews 7:25). We are not equal to Satan and the devil, the diabolos, who controls and runs this world. Quicker than the eye could recognize, quicker than a man could take a breath, would Satan destroy us were it not for the keeping intercession of our great Advocate and Mediator in glory.

But Jesus not only went inside the veil to intercede for us, but **He went to heaven to prepare a place for us (John 14:3). And these years and now these centuries, the hand of our Savior is fashioning what no architect in this life could ever dream or think of.**

He is building—He is building a city and a home for us in glory, and its size is tremendous. *"And the angel measured it, and it measured twelve thousand stadia,"* the English, *"furlongs;"* in American, one thousand five hundred miles. It is a city as though it began in Maine and went all the way down to Florida. It is so vast in its length, its breadth, and its height, that the city of God would cover all of Ireland, all of England, all of Great Britain, all of France, all of Spain, all of Germany, all of Austria, all of Italy, all of Europe and Turkey, and half of great Russia.

Fifteen hundred miles one way, fifteen hundred miles the other way, and fifteen hundred miles upward—street upon street and story upon story—the beautiful golden city of the glory and presence of God: our home in heaven, its size.

And the angel measured with the measure of a man. **He measured the walls at one hundred forty-four cubits high, about two hundred and fifty feet high, and it sits upon a great, solid foundation (Revelation 21:17). As the city descends out of heaven from God and is set down upon this earth, there is that tremendous wall and the vast cube of a foundation on which the great, mighty, holy city rests.**

CHAPTER EIGHT

And that leads me to say a second thing about the outside of the city. Will you notice its variegated, multiplied, glorious colors? God must like color. For example, do you ever see the sun set in the evening, and the clouds are burning with fire and there's gold, and there's red, and there's crimson, and there's orange, and there's blue, and there's the riot of the rainbow in the sunset?

Is there a man who ever lived who could tell us any earthly, utilitarian use for a sunset? Do you eat them? Do you buy them? Do you trade them? Can you plow them? Can you water with them? **What good is a sunset?** Just this: that God loves glorious color and things beautiful. So it is with His holy city. I cannot conceive of the riot of color in that incomparable city of God. All of these that are named here, the diamond and the sapphire, the cha/lce/dony, and the emerald, the sardonyx and the sardius, the chrysolite and the beryl, the topaz, and the chrysoprasus, the jacinth, and the amethyst (Revelation 21:19-21); God took the azure blue of the chalice of His sky, God took the surf of the raging sea, God took the emerald of the verdant meadows, He took the glory of the autumnal fall, He took the fire of an August sunset, and He crystallized it into emerald and sapphire and diamond and jasper. **Oh, what color, what beauty—God and His holy city!**

And its symmetry: God loves form, and God loves beauty, and God loves proportion. And you do, too; you don't realize it. Could you imagine a man making a crooked column, a column that leaned this way or leaned that way, or screwed around that way? Could you imagine that? Wouldn't it violate something on the inside of you, if you were to see a column looking like that, or screwed around like that? A column has to be symmetrical and proportionate and straight!

Well, where did you get that? **That's God!** That's just a little piece of the Lord's image in you. God loves things beautiful and symmetrical and proportionate.

IS THE END NEAR???

That's why the life of our Lord is so incomparably precious. He was symmetrical and proportionate, without flaw in all of His life and His personality, His mind and His heart, His soul, His affection, His will, His desires, the physical manhood, the house in which He lived. Our home in heaven is like that: beautiful and proportionate and symmetrical. And our lives are just the same.

The holy city of God—oh, where do these moments fly? Now we enter the city, we go inside of it—and we must hasten—we go inside of the beautiful city through one of the gates made out of solid pearl (Revelation 21:21). You could preach a sermon on pearl. **Enter through sufferings and through travail, through redemption, through blood and agony, through the cross; a pearl is a jewel made by a little animal that is wounded, and without the wound, the pearl is never formed. We enter heaven through gates of pearl.** And the streets of the city are pure—no defilement, pure like gold—but look like transparent glass.

"And I saw no temple therein: for the Lord God Almighty and the Lamb are the temple of it" (Revelation 21:22), no need for a temple in heaven, for the city itself is a sanctuary. God's presence is there. No temple—no need of veils, and curtains, and ceremonies, and rites, and altars, and expiation, and atonement, and covenants, and arks, and intermediators—no need for those things, for we shall live in the presence of God and shall worship immediately and directly. It shall be *Jehovah Shammah*, <u>the Lord's presence itself</u>.

No need for a temple, for God is there as He was in the garden of Eden, and this is paradise restored and regained. And the Lord God is there, and we don't need a temple. We shall see Him face to face.

CHAPTER EIGHT

"And the city had no need of the sun, nor of the moon... for the glory of God did lighten it, and the Lamb is the light thereof" (Revelation 21:23), the glory of God is His—the glory of God is His garments. It is the iridescent, it is the incomparable fusion of beauty, and color, and splendor, and life that stream from His presence. When Moses talked to God, came down from the mountainside, he wist not that his face shone. He had been with God (Exodus 34:33-35).

On the Mount of Transfiguration, the face of our Lord became bright, above the glory of the sun (Matthew 17:1-2). And when Paul on the road to Damascus met the Lord, above the light of that sidereal orb that shines in the sky did he see the light of the glory of God in the face of Jesus Christ! (Acts 22:6-7).

There is an inherent beauty and wondering life and glory in the city because Jesus is there, *"and the Lamb is the light thereof"* (Revelation 21:23). Oh, light and glory and hope and blessed strength from His blessed face! From the beginning in Genesis to the last benediction in the Revelation, it is Jesus as He was then, is now, and ever shall be, world without end. Amen! Amen!

And these who walk on its streets and live in the city are those written in the Lamb's Book of Life (Luke 10:20; Revelation 20:12, 15). And now he has a remarkable, a remarkable parallel here between what he sees in the paradise of God, in the beautiful city, and what is described in the first and the second chapter of the Book of Genesis:

> *"And he showed me a pure river of the water of life, clear as crystal...and in the midst of the street of it, and on either side of the river, was there the tree of life, which bare twelve manner of fruits"* (Revelation 22:1-2).

IS THE END NEAR???

The water of life and the manna of God, a pure river of the water of life: in Eden there was a beautiful river that had four branches, and it watered the garden. And here is the river of life. As the psalmist said, **"There is a river, the streams whereof make glad the city of God"** (Psalm 46:4).

There is nothing so refreshing as cool, clear water—that beautiful stream in the city of God. And a man drinks thereof and lives forever. And by the side of the stream flowing through the midst of the streets of the city is the tree of life in numerous specimens. You are not to think that there is just one tree of life, but the picture is that the streets are lining the river with the trees of life. It's the same kind of a thing as Longfellow speaks of in the first verse of his poem of *"Evangeline:"* which says, *"This is the forest primeval, the murmuring pine and the hemlock."* Longfellow does not mean to say just one pine and one hemlock—the forest primeval, the murmuring pine and hemlock, its specimen throughout the great forest. **So the tree of life, in numerous specimens lining the river, and the manna thereof and the food and fruit thereof are for the nourishment of God's immortal saints. It means you're going to eat in heaven; you're going to eat in heaven.** We've spoken of that with delight and anticipation. Going to eat in heaven—nothing about that I object to. Going to eat in heaven: the angels ate when they were entertained by Abraham. Our Lord Jesus ate when He was raised from the dead (Luke 24:41-43). He said, **"But I say unto you, I will not drink henceforth of this fruit of the vine, until that day when I drink it new with you in my Father's kingdon."** (Matthew 26:29).

We're going to be at the marriage supper of the Lamb (Revelation 19:6-9). We're going to eat! There are twelve manner of

CHAPTER EIGHT

fruit that come every month on those trees. I wonder what it will taste like, the ambrosia of God. Oh, the fellowship and the gladness of such a thing as God hath prepared for us!

But we hasten. "The throne of God and the Lamb shall be in it; and His servants shall serve Him" (Revelation 22:3). How many times do you hear people, as someone said to me last week, **"I can't imagine heaven being interesting—just sit and sit and do nothing and nothing and nothing?"** There is no intimation that heaven is such a thing as that.

In the Garden of Eden, before the man was made, God said He needed somebody to till the ground, and when He made the man, He placed him in the garden that he might dress it and keep it. And he was to have dominion over things above and things around him and things below it. There was a tremendous assignment and responsibility for the first man in the garden of Eden (Genesis 1:28; 2:16).

And every indication you have of what it is like over there in the glory that is yet to come is of that same thing. For example, in the parable of the pounds, when He blessed that man who had made ten pounds, He said: *"Now, you shall have authority over ten cities."* And when this man had made five pounds, He said: *"You shall have authority over five cities"* (Luke 19:17-19).

There is a great administration over there in the future kingdom of God in heaven. There are nations here that are mentioned. There is government. There are assignments. There are responsibilities. And we shall all live in that beautiful and incomparably precious civilization. **And each man shall have his place according to his faithfulness and reward in this world and in this life.**

IS THE END NEAR???

"And His servants shall serve Him." And in the most climactic and meaningful of all, *"And they shall see His face; and His name shall be in their foreheads"* (Revelation 22:3-4). This is what it is to be in heaven: to look upon the face of God, our Lord, and to be with one another and live. **That is heaven!**

Incidentally, gates of pearl; incidentally, streets of gold; incidentally, a wall of jasper—mostly and foremost, our *LORD* and one another.

I can hear the Lord as He would say to you: **"On what street would you like to live in glory, and what mansion would you like to call your home?"** And I can hear a true saint reply: **"Dear Lord, any street, any mansion, just so the windows open on the palace of the great King, that I might see Him come and go."** Isn't that a sentiment that strikes a chord in your heart? **"Any street, Lord, any house, Lord, just so I might see Thy blessed and precious face and that we might be together in heaven."**

Blind Fanny Crosby wrote a song like that that's in your hymnbook. She entitled it: "My Savior, First of All." We rarely ever sing it any more, but when I was a boy, we sang it all of the time.

> *When my life work is ended,*
> *And I cross the swelling tide,*
> *When the bright and glorious morning I shall see;*
> *I shall know my Redeemer*
> *When I reach the other side,*
> *And His smile will be the first to welcome me.*
> *Through the gates of the city*
> *In a robe of spotless white,*
> *He will lead me where no tears will ever fall;*
> *In the glad song of the ages*
> *I shall mingle with delight,*
> *But I long to see my Savior first of all.*

CHAPTER EIGHT

"And they shall see His face; His name shall be in their foreheads, and they shall reign and live forever and ever, amen (Revelation 22:4-5)! Amen!

**THIS, DEAR CHRISTIAN, IS GLORY!!!!
THIS IS OUR ETERNAL HOME!!!!**

<u>NOW THEN</u>: John sees a whole new creation spring into being.

Now read Revelation 21:1-10. **OH!** What beautiful words! **They bring us full circle, to the beginning of the Bible again.** Genesis 1:1 says, *"In the beginning God created the heavens and the earth."* That creation is what is called here "the old heavens and the old earth." They shall pass away, as we are told, but a new heaven and a new earth is coming. It is the Apostle Peter who tells us what happens to the present heavens and earth. In Second Peter he says, *"But the day of the Lord will come like a thief. The heavens will disappear with a roar. The elements will be destroyed by fire, and the earth and everything in it will be laid bare,"* (2 Peter 3:10 - NIV). That ends the old heavens, but now a new heaven and earth appear where Jesus will continue his reign, not only upon earth, but throughout the entire reach of the vast universe of God.

<u>There are four statements in this opening paragraph that tell us the purpose of the new heavens and the new earth:</u>

1. The first two verses suggests strongly that the New Jerusalem, this great city that John describes, **is to be the capital of the whole new universe**. And it will be a universe greatly changed. It will not be like the one we have now. I do not believe that this means that God will eliminate the present heavens and earth but He changes it and cleanses it. **When we become Christians we become new creatures in Christ, but we are still the same persons, but now**

IS THE END NEAR???

changed and cleansed. So also the old heavens and the old earth will be cleansed -- by fire. We know today that the present universe in its farthest reaches (even farther than any discovered telescope can show us), is governed by the same laws. One of them is the Second Law of Thermodynamics, the law of entropy (measure of chaos), which says this present universe is running down. It is all decaying; losing its energy; it is growing cold.

- ❖ But in the new heavens and the new earth that law is reversed. Instead of running down the universe begins to come together again. Instead of losing energy it will gain it and manifest a unity, stability, symmetry and beauty that the old heavens and earth never had. One aspect of this, pictured here, is that there will be no more sea. A man once said to a well known preacher, "I don't think I'm going to like the new heavens and the new earth, because I love the ocean." To which the preacher said, "I understand that feeling. I love the ocean too."

- ❖ But do you realize that the one reason <u>we have a salt sea that covers more than half of this planet is because it is God's great antiseptic to cleanse the earth and make life possible on earth</u>. Had it not been for the ocean, and the salt in it particularly, life on this planet would have ceased many centuries ago. It is the ocean that purges, cleanses, and preserves it. The sea is an antiseptic in which all the pollution and filth that man pours into it is absorbed, cleansed and changed. But there will be no more pollution, no more filth, no more need for cleansing in the new universe. <u>Though we are not told this, I think there</u>

CHAPTER EIGHT

<u>will be large bodies of fresh water, larger even perhaps than the Great Lakes, that we may enjoy in the new heavens and new earth</u>.

2. The second thing said here is, the New Jerusalem is called a bride beautifully dressed for her husband. Everyone loves that picture. We all love weddings. The climax is when the bride comes down the aisle, beautifully dressed for her husband! Everyone forgets that poor fellow waiting for her at the altar! Every eye is on the bride because she has prepared herself for weeks to meet her husband there. **This new city is called both a city and a woman**, just as the false bride, "Mystery Babylon the Great," was both a city (Rome), and a woman. **We have seen how that one was destroyed for its evil.**

   A bride speaks of intimacy, and a city speaks of community. So we have a picture here of the redeemed of God, **each one given a body of glory empowered with limitless energy.** When opportunity comes in that day you will not say, as we often say today, *"The spirit is willing but the flesh is weak,"* (Matthew 26:41).

   No, then you will be able to respond to every opportunity with a glorified, fresh and living body. We will live in close intimacy, not only with the Lord himself, but with each other as well. I often think of that phrase in John's letters where he says, *"It does not yet appear what we shall be,"* (1 John 3:2 KJV). I keep looking in the mirror for signs of change in me. But what do I see? Wrinkles--and welllllllllll! But it won't be like that then. **We will have bodies of glory and beauty that will be like His.**

3. The third thing we are told here is that this will be the dwelling place of God. **Isn't that wonderful? The home of God! The place where God lives**, in his people. This is when the name "Immanuel"

IS THE END NEAR???

("God with us"), will be fulfilled, and when the New Covenant will be fully worked out, *"They shall be my people, and I will be their God,"* (Jeremiah 24:7 KJV). It is all in this beautiful setting. Heaven, someone has well said, is the place of "no more" - - no more death, no more sorrow, no more parting, no more pain, no more tears, no more evil! I love that old song that goes like this:

> **There's no disappointment in heaven**
> **No weariness, sorrow, no pain,**
> **No song with a minor refrain.**
> **The clouds of our earthly horizon**
> **Shall never appear in the sky.**
> **But all will be sunshine and gladness,**
> **With never a sob nor a sigh**

A wonderful hope, isn't it? It is so beautiful that it is even hard to believe. I think John felt that way for he is given at this point certain words of assurance to help him with his possible doubt.

He who was seated on the throne said, *"I am making everything new!"* Then he said, "Write this down, for these words are trustworthy and true." He said to me: *"It is done. I am the Alpha and the Omega, the Beginning and the End"* (Revelation 21:5-6a).

He brackets all of time in the phrases, "I am the Alpha and the Omega, the Beginning and the End." Everything in between comes from him. **These are words of truth that help us to believe.**

Remember on the cross our Lord uttered the words *"It is finished,"* (John 19:30). After the gloom, the darkness, pain, sorrow and anguish of his separation from the Father, he cried out, "It is finished!" The basis of redemption was settled. The sacrifice was ended. The basis was fully laid. Now he says, **"It is done!"** Redemption is complete. The

CHAPTER EIGHT

redeemed are safely home in glory. Everything that God wants done is done! Not one thing is left unfinished. The fourth thing the passage suggests as the purpose of the New Jerusalem is that it will be the home of the redeemed: Revelation 21:6b-7- - - **What wonderful words!**

This city will be the home of the redeemed, and the only qualification for it is that you be thirsty. Nothing on earth satisfies. Wealth, fame, pleasures and treasures - - none will meet that deep thirst of the soul. That is why the rich, the wealthy, the beautiful people, all are looking for something more. They are not satisfied.

But here is the promise to satisfy that thirst. People who want more - - who want God - - **are promised that they shall drink of the water of the spring of life**. <u>These are also called "overcomers" who "inherit all this," all that God has created</u>. Peter tells us in his first letter that there is waiting for us *"an inheritance that can never perish, spoil or fade, kept in heaven for us,"* (1 Peter 1:4 NIV). Those who are thus changed by God's grace and love are to be forever his sons. That includes all female believers as well! You godly women and girls have always had the right to call yourself a son of God because he is *"bringing many sons to glory."* So we shall all be sons of God in that day. Now, by contrast, in a reference back to what we have seen of the judgment there is in Verse 8 a description of those who are not admitted:

"But the cowardly, the unbelieving, the vile, the murderers, the sexually immoral, those who practice magic arts, the idolaters and all liars-they will be consigned to the fiery lake of burning sulfur. This is the second death" (Revelation 21:8 NIV).

As we have seen all through this book, God does not want that. He is very reluctant that anybody should be judged or condemned, but as the word points out, **"they judge themselves."** Here there are three attitudes of heart which result in five visible deeds that mark the lost. The three attitudes are the reasons why some will miss this beautiful city.

First, the cowards, i.e. the fearful, those who are afraid to take on the yoke of Christ, who fear to confess Christ, who are unwilling to be unpopular for a little while. They shrug their shoulders and turn away from the offer of life. Secondly, there are the unbelieving, those who know it is true, but don't want it and refuse the evidence, deliberately turning their backs on truth. Third, there are the vile. The word means "to become foul." You do not start out that way, but by feeding your mind with filthy things - - foul literature, filthy attitudes and actions, you become foul-minded. If any of these are your attitude, then out of it will flow murders, fornication, adultery, occult practices, and finally, hypocritical living. Jesus warned of that - - those who profess to be Christians but really there is no change in their lives. None who practice these activities will be in the city of God. In these eight verses we have looked at the purpose of the New Jerusalem. Now John is given another vision of it and describes it in wonderfully symbolic language as the great city of God: First, we are informed as to the structure of this city.

One of the seven angels who had the seven bowls full of the seven last plagues came and said to me, "Come, I will show you the bride, the wife of the Lamb." And he carried me away in the Spirit to a mountain great and high, and showed me the Holy City, Jerusalem, coming down out of heaven from God. It shone with the glory of God, and its brilliance was like that of a very precious jewel, like a jasper, clear as crystal. It had a great, high wall with twelve gates, and with twelve angels at the gates. On the gates were written the names of the

CHAPTER EIGHT

twelve tribes of Israel. There were three gates on the east, three on the north, three on the south and three on the west. The wall of the city had twelve foundations, and on them were the names of the twelve apostles of the Lamb (Revelation 21:9-14 NIV).

I am sure someone is asking, "Is this literal or is it symbolic?" I hope, by now, as we have been going through this book, you have come to realize that you do not have to make that choice. God loves to use literal things that remain symbols. The cross behind me is literal (i.e., the cross mounted behind the pulpit at MBC), but it is also a symbol of the death of Jesus. It is both at the same time. So, all through this book, we find the blending of the literal and symbolic. I believe there will be a great, visible city of incredible brilliance and glory, located somewhere above or within the atmosphere of the earth, which also will picture activities and relationships that are going on within the community of the saints. Those will be characterized by stability, by symmetry, by light, by life and ministry. That is what is described here. The literal is very evident; the symbolic perhaps needs a bit of interpretation.

The high wall of the city speaks of separation and of intimacy. If you want to have an intimate garden party, you meet in the yard behind a wall. That wall shuts out other things and people. It speaks of intimate fellowship and separation from intrusion. The whole of Scripture with one voice speaks of God's desire to have what He calls "a people for my own possession." Everything in the universe is, in a sense, His possession. All animals, all creatures, are His. There are billions of angels and they all belong to Him. But the saints are peculiarly God's own possession. That is because He has made them to correspond to Himself. He can share with them the deepest things in His life and in His heart. They satisfy Him and fulfill Him just as a bride satisfies and fulfills her husband.

IS THE END NEAR???

The gates describe means of access and egress from the city. There is an amazing verse in John 10 where Jesus says, **"Whoever enters through me will be saved, and he will go in and out and find pasture,"** (John 10:9 NIV). That seems to be a portrayal of the widespread ministry of believers throughout the eternal ages. The new universe will surely be as big or bigger than it is now -- and it is mind-blowing in its immensity now! Billions of galaxies, far larger than our own galaxy of the Milky Way, fill the heavens as far as the eye can see by means of the greatest telescopes we have, and still we have not reached the end. That means that there will be new planets to develop, new principles to discover, new joys to experience. Every moment of eternity will be an adventure of discovery. Those gates are named for the tribes of Israel. It is a perpetual reminder that **"salvation is of the Jews,"** (John 4:22 KJV). Access to the city is through Israel. I believe that pictures the truth that has come to us through the Old Testament prophets and the godly practices of the nation. Many of these brilliant passages that now intrigue, but puzzle us, will come to life then as we have never known them before. They will lead us out to new adventures that we have never dreamed of in our wildest imaginations.

The foundations speak of what is underneath which gives stability and permanence. They are named for the 12 apostles. Judas, of course, was replaced in the apostolic band by Matthias as we are told in the first chapter of Acts. These foundations speak of New Testament truth and practice. Things that we only faintly grasp now will be wonderfully understood and experienced then, especially the three things that abide forever: faith, hope, and love! **"These three,"** says Paul, **"and the greatest of these is love,"** (1 Corinthians 13:13). It beggars language to describe this. I find myself stumbling and unable to express fully the beauty that is portrayed here, but I hope that the inner

CHAPTER EIGHT

eye of your imagination will make much of it. Now we are given the measurements of the city.

The angel who talked with me had a measuring rod of gold to measure the city, its gates and its walls. The city was laid out like a square, as long as it was wide. He measured the city with the rod and found it to be 12,000 stadia in length, and as wide and as high as it is long [that is about 1500 miles]. He measured its wall and it was 144 cubits thick, by man's measurement, which the angel was using (Revelation 21:15-17 NIV).

When God measures something it is a sign of his ownership. The number 12, which is everywhere in this account - - 12,000 stadia, 144 cubits (that is 12 times 12) wide - - is in Scripture the number of government. So this is a fulfillment of that wonderful word in Isaiah, *"the government shall be upon his shoulder, and his name shall be called Wonderful, Counsellor, the Mighty God, the Everlasting Father, the Prince of Peace,"* (Isaiah 9:6 KJV). It is a city of beauty and of symmetry, just as long as it is wide, just as tall as it is long. I do not think you need think of that as a cube; it is more probably a pyramid. It will be a city of perfect proportions. That is what it symbolizes - - perfectly proportioned wholeness!

Everybody wants that. Everyone wants to be a whole person. People say, **"I want to be me. I want to fulfill myself. I want to get my act together."** Many pick the wrong way to do it. They think that it is all up to them. The one message of the Word of God is that you cannot find your own way. Try to fulfill yourself and you will lose yourself. But if you let God fulfill you, then you will be fully filled - - a wholeness perfectly proportioned, containing nothing awkward, nothing out of balance, but all in harmony. Our friend, Eugene Peterson, whom I have quoted many times in this study, has put it well. He says,

> "The two symbolic cities of the Apocalypse, Babylon and Jerusalem, show [how a wall creates group consciousness and interrelatedness]. When evil reaches its highest density it forms a whore - city. That city is a concentrate of evil and is destroyed. Likewise, when God - consciousness and the interrelatedness of love reach their highest density, a bride - city is formed.
>
> Not only is the size and shape of the city revealed, but the materials from which it is made are given to us."

The wall was made of jasper [imagine a great diamond shining in the sun], and the city of pure gold, as pure as glass. The foundations of the city walls were decorated with every kind of precious stone. The first foundation was jasper, the second sapphire, the third chalcedony, the fourth emerald, the fifth sardonyx, the sixth carnelian, the seventh chrysolite, the eighth beryl, the ninth topaz, the tenth chrysoprase, the eleventh jacinth, and the twelfth amethyst. The twelve gates were twelve pearls, each gate made of a single pearl. The street of the city was of pure gold, like transparent glass (Revelation 21:18-21 NIV).

Let your imagination picture that marvelous city - - gleaming transparent gold, with foundations sparkling with light in cascading colors, pouring forth from great jewels embedded in the sides - - a kaleidoscope of light and glory! What are those foundations? As we have already seen, they are the twelve apostles. This then portrays the truth that the apostolic revelation is filled with light. There is a verse in Ephesians 3 where the Apostle Paul speaks of ***"the manifold***

CHAPTER EIGHT

wisdom of God that is to be made known by the church to rulers and authorities in heavenly places," (Ephesians 3:10). That is describing this same phenomena. The word "manifold" is literally "many-colored," - - the many-colored wisdom of God - - fresh wisdom flashing from old truth from the apostles.

The gates are made of single pearls. You have heard many jokes about St. Peter and the pearly gates, which we usually conceive of as a single great pair of gates. But there are twelve gates, each one is a gigantic pearl, and St. Peter is nowhere to be seen at any of them! God must have some huge oysters somewhere in this new universe for each gate is but a single pearl! Pearls speak of beauty out of pain. Beauty comes from pain in an oyster. I have a message I preached years ago on the parable of the Pearl of Great Price. I called it The Case of the Irritated Oyster, because a pearl is formed when a tiny grain of sand gets inside an oyster's shell and the oyster becomes very uncomfortable. It feels like crackers in bed. To relieve its pain it covers the irritant with a soft lustrous nacre that hardens into a beautiful, glowing pearl. It describes beautifully how the redeemed come from the pain of Jesus. He was the husbandman who came looking for a pearl of great price. He found one, a beautiful pearl which came out of the pain that he suffered as he went through the terrible anguish of the cross. Out of that pain came the church of Jesus Christ, the pearl of great price. He sold all that he had to buy it. This means that the redeemed will never forget for all eternity the pain and shame of the cross of Christ. They will sing forever,

> *In the cross of Christ I glory,*
> *Towering o'er the wrecks of time.*
> *All the light of sacred story*
> *Gathers round its head sublime.*

IS THE END NEAR???

THE TRANSCENDENT LIGHT
OF THIS CITY IS DESCRIBED NEXT

I did not see a temple in the city, because the Lord God Almighty and the Lamb are its temple. The city does not need the sun or the moon to shine on it, for the glory of God gives it light, and the Lamb is its lamp. The nations will walk by its light, and the kings of the earth will bring their splendor into it. On no day will its gates ever be shut, for there will be no night there. The glory and honor of the nations will be brought into it. Nothing impure will ever enter it, nor will anyone who does what is shameful or deceitful, but only those whose names are written in the Lamb's book of life" (Revelation 21:22-27 NIV).

All through Revelation we have seen a temple in heaven described. That temple remains throughout the millennium, as the original of which the earthly temple is a copy. But in the new heavens and earth there is no temple. Why? Because the true temple, of which the one in the old heavens is a picture, is the True Man, Jesus himself. God in man that is the temple! Thus Paul, in First Corinthians, says, "Do you not know that your body is a temple of the Holy Spirit, who is in you?" (1 Corinthians 6:19a NIV). If God dwells in you, you are a part of this heavenly temple. You share the honor of being the home of God, the dwelling place of God. And from that comes radiant light. People can see all things by that truth. So glorious is it that there is no need for the sun or the moon. It does not say they are not there; it simply says there is no need for them in this city of God. There will never be night there because it is lit continually by the glory which is God in man. The gates will never be shut because there is no night there and therefore

CHAPTER EIGHT

no need for protection. Cities close their gates at night because they are in danger. But there is nothing to destroy in this new world to come. The kings of the earth will bring their glory in, not to compete with the glory of God, but to have it revealed by the light of God. Nothing impure will enter because only the redeemed are admitted. Finally, the life of this city is described in the opening words of chapter 22:

"Then the angel showed me the river of the water of life, as clear as crystal, flowing from the throne of God and of the Lamb down the middle of the great street of the city. On each side of the river stood the tree of life, bearing twelve crops of fruit, yielding its fruit every month. And the leaves of the tree are for the health [not healing, as translated in the NIV] of the nations. No longer will there be any curse. The throne of God and of the Lamb will be in the city, and his servants will serve him. They will see his face, and his name will be on their foreheads. There will be no more night. They will not need the light of a lamp or the light of the sun, for the Lord God will give them light. And they will reign for ever and ever" (Revelation 22:1-5 NIV).

What a glorious picture of abounding fertility, of life on every side -- a river of life, a tree of life. Both of these are found in the Old Testament. Psalm 46 says, "There is a river that makes glad the city of God," (Psalm 46:4a). Ezekiel describes a river flowing out from the throne of God. It is a wonderful river to swim in, he said. The tree of life is found in the Garden of Eden. It is right there, along with the tree of the knowledge of good and evil. But here it is back again.

The river symbolizes the Holy Spirit. Jesus said on one occasion of those who believe in him, "out of his innermost being

IS THE END NEAR???

shall flow rivers of living water," (John 7:38 KJV). John comments, "This he said of the Spirit, which those who believe on him should receive," (John 7:39 KJV). The tree is a symbol of Jesus himself. He is the way, the truth and the life, the tree of life. When we obey the Word of God we are eating and feeding on Jesus and drawing life from that nourishment. That is what this signifies. It brings spiritual health. We flourish when we follow his word and obey and live by it. No wonder that from this magnificent scene of life there flow three wonderful ministries: First, empowered service. His servants will serve him. There is nothing they could ask for more than that; there is no greater pleasure or joy than the service of God. And they will be in intimate fellowship -- they will see his face, and bear his name, just as a bride bears her husband's name and sees his face. And they will have enlightened authority. They shall reign forever and ever. Do you think heaven is going to be boring? No, boredom is a sign of selfishness. When you are bored, it is because you are selfish. You want someone to do something for you; you want some excitement to minister to you. But all selfishness will be ended then, and therefore there will be no boredom in heaven. There is continual excitement, discovery, anticipation -- and constant gratitude and praise. The rest of the book is simply an epilogue. As the book began with a prologue, so it ends with an epilogue. It consists mostly of assurances. Many people neglect the book of Revelation. They distrust it and do not understand it. They need reassurance that it comes from God and speaks the truth. So the epilogue is made up of assurances, the first one from "the God of the spirits of the prophets."

The angel said to me, "These words are trustworthy and true. The Lord, the God who inspires the prophets, sent his angel to show his servants the things that must soon take place" (Revelation 22:6 NIV).

CHAPTER EIGHT

There is a guarantee right from God himself that these words are to be believed. They are trustworthy and true. Then an assurance from Jesus himself.

"Behold, I am coming soon! Blessed is he who keeps the words of the prophecy in this book" (**Revelation 22:7 NIV**).

Read it, study it, keep it, he says. You will be blessed and strengthened by it, and made ready to meet him when he comes. Then there follows a word from John:

"I, John, am the one who heard and saw these things. And when I had heard and seen them, I fell down to worship at the feet of the angel who had been showing them to me. But he said to me, "Do not do it! I am a fellow servant with you and with your brothers the prophets and of all who keep the words of this book. Worship God!" (**Revelation 22:8-9 NIV**).

We have an account like this in Chapter 19 where the same thing is recorded. Personally I do not believe that John made the same mistake twice. I think here he is referring back to what he did in Chapter 19. He is reminding us how he reacted when he heard all these things. He says, in effect, "When I had heard them and seen them I was so confused, so uncertain, and so overwhelmed that I fell down to worship at the angel's feet." He is recounting his most embarrassing moment, and reminding us that it was quite the wrong reaction. Let it lead you, rather, to worship God. When you read this book, open your heart and praise the God of glory who gives us such a fantastic future as that described here. Then there is another word from the angel:

IS THE END NEAR???

Then he told me, *"Do not seal up the words of the prophecy of this book, because the time is near. Let him who does wrong continue to do wrong; let him who is vile continue to be vile; let him who does right continue to do right; and let him who is holy continue to be holy"* (Revelation 22:10-11 NIV).

That is a reminder again that each day we are working out one of two separate destinies. Either we are on the right track, following the Lord, walking with him, doing right, or we have already made a choice for wrong and our lives are falling apart. If that is the course you are determined on, then evil is what will follow. There is no other escape than the way of faith in Christ. You will have to continue the way you are going. Then a reassuring word comes from Jesus again,

"Behold, I am coming soon! My reward is with me, and I will give to everyone according to what he has done. I am the Alpha and the Omega, the First and the Last, the Beginning and the End" (Revelation 22:12-13 NIV).

That is a wonderful renewal of his promise that when he comes, all this shall become true. The next word is a reminder of the two destinies once again.

"Blessed are those who wash their robes, that they may have the right to the tree of life and may go through the gates into the city. Outside are the dogs [that is an ancient word for those who practice homosexuality], those who practice magic arts, the sexually immoral, the murderers, the idolaters and everyone who loves and practices falsehood[that is, those who pretend to be something they are not]" (Revelation 22:14-15 NIV).

CHAPTER EIGHT

That is a most solemn warning, a reminder that what we do and believe from day to day is leading us in one direction or the other. Then yet another word from Jesus:

> *"I, Jesus, have sent my angel to give you this testimony for the churches. I am the Root and the Offspring of David [he is the root from which David came, and he is also David's son], and the bright Morning Star [the one who promises to come for his own before the Son of Righteousness arises]" (Revelation 22:16 NIV).*

Notice the many times through this closing section we have the promise that Jesus is coming soon. Many people read that and say, "How can that be? This was said centuries ago." Some even say, "John and the other apostles were wrong. They said he was coming soon, but 2,000 years have gone by and he still hasn't come. It shows how wrong this book is." But if you read this book remembering that it is a book that links time and eternity together, you will understand that everything here, either the destiny of the lost or the destiny of the righteous, takes place the minute you die. It is never any further away than your own personal death. That could be very soon, couldn't it? It may yet be some time before it breaks into time, but it will not be long before each of us leaves time and enters eternity. The book then closes with an invitation and another brief warning:

> *"'The Spirit and the bride say, "Come! And let him who hears say, "Come!" Whoever is thirsty, let him come; and whoever wishes, let him take the free gift of the water of life'" (Revelation 22:17 NIV).*

IS THE END NEAR???

That is the invitation. It comes from the Spirit of God individual Christian. All voices join to exhort the reader: **"Come!"** Take the free gift of life. It is waiting for all who come to Christ. Then the warning: ***(Revelation 22:18-19 NIV).***

In other words, do not change a thing! This is the truth of God. Do not change it -- do not subtract from it or add to it. It is what God says. As a symbolic book, it requires interpretation, but be careful. Do not take away its meaning by emphasizing the symbolic at the expense of the literal. Do not destroy its intent by accepting only the literal without understanding what it symbolizes. Believe it, because the final word from Jesus is:

He who testifies to these things says,
"Yes, I am coming soon" (Revelation 22:20a NIV).

So let all God's people say:

"Amen.! Come, Lord Jesus" (Revelation 22:20b NIV).

CHAPTER EIGHT

And as we close the book,
I join John the Apostle in saying to you:

"The grace of the Lord Jesus be with God's people. Amen........"

(Revelation 22:21 NIV).

IS THE END NEAR???

THOUGHTS:

_____

_____

_____

_____

_____

ACTIONS:

_____

_____

_____

_____

_____

CHAPTER NINE

WHERE IS ISRAEL IN BIBLE PROPHECY

IS THE END NEAR???

Any student of the Word of God, knows that Israel is the focus of end time Bible prophecy. That's the reason that the re-establishment of the nation on May 14, 1948 is so important. That event signaled the fact that we are now living in the end of the end times.

I. Prophecies Concerning Israel

During the 20th Century, we were privileged to witness God beginning to fulfill in whole or in part seven prophecies regarding the Jewish people:

A. The Jewish State (Isaiah 11:10-12).

The regathering of the Jews from the four corners of the earth. This was prompted by Theodor Herzl's book, *The Jewish State*, which was published in 1896. There were 40,000 Jews in Palestine in 1900. As of May 2016, there are 8,655,535 *million* in the land of Israel.

CHAPTER NINE

B. The re-establishment of the state of Israel (Ezekiel 37:21-22).

This prophecy was fulfilled on May 14, 1948 when the Israeli Declaration of Independence was proclaimed in Tel Aviv.

C. The reclamation of the land (Ezekiel 36:34-35).

When the Jews started returning to the land in the early 20th Century, it was a malaria-infested swampland that had been denuded of all its forests. Today, it is the bread basket of the Middle East, and the forests have been replanted.

D. The revival of the Hebrew language (Zephaniah 3:9 and Jeremiah 31:23).

When the Jews were scattered worldwide, they stopped speaking Hebrew. But in the 19th Century, God raised up a man in Lithuania named Eliezer Ben-Yehuda who devoted his life to resurrecting the language from the dead. In 1922, the British declared biblical Hebrew to be one of the three official languages of Palestine, together with English and Arabic. Ben-Yehuda died one month later.

E. The re-occupation of the city of Jerusalem (Zechariah 8:4-8).

When the Israeli War of Independence ended in 1949, the Old City of Jerusalem was under Jordanian occupation. The Israelis conquered the city on June 7, 1967 during the Six Day War.

F. The resurgence of the Israeli military (Zechariah 12:6).

Despite the fact that Israel is one of the smallest nations in the world, its military is regularly ranked among the top ten to fifteen in the world.

IS THE END NEAR???

G. The re-focusing of world politics on the nation of Israel and its city of Jerusalem (Zechariah 12:2-3).

Today the whole world is focused on trying to force Israel to surrender all or part of Jerusalem.

II. <u>Military Power in Prophecy</u>

Let's take an in-depth look at how one of these prophecies was fulfilled in the 20th Century and continues to be fulfilled to this day — the resurgence of the Israeli military.

The prophet Ezekiel referred to the revival of Israel in the last days as producing "an exceeding great army" (Ezekiel 37:10). Zechariah was more specific. He prophesied that God would make **"the clans of Judah like a firepot among pieces of wood and a flaming torch among sheaves,"** enabling them to **"consume on the right hand and on the left" all their enemies** (Zechariah 12:6). He proceeded to state that in the end times, the nation will be so strong that the "feeble among them in that day will be like David, and the house of David will be like God, like the angel of the Lord before them" (Zechariah 12:8).

Let's look now at the evidence of the fulfillment of these prophecies.

A. The <u>War of Independence</u> (November 1947 – March 1949)

On November 29, 1947 the United Nations adopted a resolution providing for the ending of the League of Nations Mandate for Palestine, replacing British rule with a partition of the land that would result in the creation of two states, one for the Jews and the other for the Arabs.

CHAPTER NINE

The Jews worldwide were elated, even though the piece of territory they were provided was minuscule compared to what they had been promised by the British in the Balfour Declaration in November of 1917. But the Arabs were outraged because they wanted all the land of Palestine. The result was the immediate launching of a civil war as the Arabs began to attack Jewish communities. This bloody conflict continued right up to the day that the Jews issued their Declaration of Independence on May 14, 1948.

As that epic day approached, the Arabs issued repeated warnings that they would launch an all-out war if the Jews proceeded to establish a nation. For example, the Secretary General of the Arab League, Azzam Pasha, declared, "It will be a war of annihilation. It will be a momentous massacre in history that will be talked about like the massacres of the Mongols or the Crusades."[1]

On the Jewish side, there was considerable concern that such boasting could become a reality. Thus, on the eve of the war, Yigael Yadin, the Chief of Staff of the Israeli forces, told David Ben-Gurion, the Jewish leader, "The best we can tell you is that we have a 50-50 chance."[2]

The trepidation on the part of the Jews was more than justified. Within hours of the declaration of independence on the afternoon of May 14, 1948, five Arab armies began invading the new nation (Egypt, Syria, Transjordan, Lebanon and Iraq). The Israeli forces consisted at most of 30,000 rag-tag underground fighters who were ill-trained and poorly equipped. (The Israeli Defense Force, known as the IDF, was not organized until after the invasion.)

The Arab armies, particularly the Jordanians, were well equipped and trained. Egypt, Iraq and Syria had air forces. Egypt and Syria also had tank forces. All had modern artillery. The troops of Transjordan were led by a British officer, General John Glubb.[3]

IS THE END NEAR???

Although the United States recognized the new state of Israel immediately, the Truman Administration did not provide any aid. Instead, Truman declared an arms embargo under the naive assumption that it would help avert bloodshed. Meanwhile, the British gladly supplied arms openly to the Arabs, while Israel had to smuggle weapons purchased in Czechoslovakia.

But despite the overwhelming odds against them, the infant Jewish state prevailed. The cost was enormous. A total of 6,377 Israelis were killed, representing nearly one percent of the population (equivalent to an American loss today of three million!). But the Israelis ended up not only with the territory that had been allotted to them by the UN, but also with control of 60% of the area that had been proposed for an Arab state. Arab casualties totaled between 8,000 and 15,000, and they ended up with only 22% of the total territory of Palestine.[4]

The only key area that the Israelis were unable to conquer was the Old City of Jerusalem. Overall, the war resulted in an incredible victory for Israel.

During the war there were many miraculous events. One occurred at a kibbutz (collective farm) called Yad Mordecai, located 36 miles south of Tel Aviv near the northern border of the Gaza Strip. The kibbutz was located on the coastal road from Egypt to Tel Aviv.

The Egyptian army, composed of 5,000 troops, divided as it moved north. Half the troops headed for Jerusalem, the other 2,500 continued north toward Tel Aviv. The latter unit arrived at Yad Mordecai on May 19. They were heavily armed, and they were backed up with tanks, artillery and air support.[5]

The kibbutz evacuated all its children and most of its women as they prepared for the Egyptian attack. They were left with 130

CHAPTER NINE

defenders (110 kibbutzniks and 20 fighters from Tel Aviv). They dug trenches and reinforced them with sand bags. Their armament consisted of 37 rifles, one anti-tank gun, two light mortars and two machine guns.[6]

There was no hope for the kibbutz, and its defenders were well aware of that fact. But they bravely dug in and prepared to take what appeared to be a suicidal stand.

The Egyptians attacked furiously with ground troops, tank assaults, artillery barrages, and air sorties. Incredibly, the Yad Mordecai defenders held out for five days! The Egyptians were not able to overrun the kibbutz until the defenders decided to retreat under the cover of darkness due to the fact that half of them had either been killed or incapacitated.[7]

Over 300 Egyptian soldiers died in the battle, and the five days gave the defender of Tel Aviv time to prepare their defenses. Also, during that time, four Messerschmitt airplanes had arrived from Czechoslovakia and had been hastily assembled. They were used on May 29 to stop the Egyptian army before it could reach Tel Aviv.[8]

How could 130 untrained civilians with only rudimentary armament hold off the Egyptian army for five days? No one has ever been able to explain it.

B. The Six Day War (June 1967)

In the early 1960s, Gamal Abdel Nasser, the President of Egypt, decided to try to establish his nation as the leader of the Arab world. Part of that strategy was the demonization of Israel in his public speeches. He also encouraged terrorist attacks against Israel.

IS THE END NEAR???

In 1965 Nasser asserted, "We shall not enter Palestine with its soil covered in sand; we shall enter it with its soil saturated in blood."[9] A few months later, Nasser declared that he had two aims. "The immediate aim: perfection of Arab military might. The national aim: the eradication of Israel."[10]

On May 15, 1967, Nasser started moving Egyptian troops into the Sinai desert, massing them near the Israeli border. He then ordered the UN troops in the buffer zone between Israel and Egypt to leave. When the UN readily complied, he announced:[11]

"As of today, there no longer exists an international emergency force to protect Israel. We shall exercise patience no more. We shall not complain any more to the UN about Israel. The sole method we shall apply against Israel is total war, which will result in the extermination of Zionist existence."

The Syrian Defense Minister, Hafez Assad, replied enthusiastically: "The Syrian army, with its finger on the trigger, is united… [and] I, as a military man, believe that the time has come to enter into a battle of annihilation."[12]

On May 22, Egypt blockaded the Straits of Tiran to all Israel shipping — an action considered to be an act of war under international law. At that point, Nasser began to challenge Israel daily to fight. On May 28, he declared, "We will not accept any… coexistence with Israel."[13]

King Hussein of Jordan signed a defense pact with Egypt on May 30, and Nasser announced.

The armies of Egypt, Jordan, Syria and Lebanon are poised on the borders of Israel… while standing behind us are the armies

CHAPTER NINE

of Iraq, Algeria, Kuwait, Sudan and the whole Arab nation…the critical hour has arrived. We have reached the stage of serious action and not declarations.

President Abdur Rahman Aref of Iraq joined in the war of words, declaring, "Our goal is clear — to wipe Israel off the map."[15]

The Arab rhetoric was matched by the mobilization of forces. Approximately 465,000 troops, together with 2,800 tanks and 800 aircraft were assembled for the attack on Israel.[16]

The Israeli leaders decided it would be suicidal to wait for the attack, and so, on June 5, Prime Minister Levi Eshkol gave the order to launch a preemptive attack on Egypt. The entire Israeli Air Force, with the exception of 12 planes assigned to defend Israel's air space, took off in the early morning, and in less than two hours they destroyed over 300 Egyptian aircraft sitting on the ground. A few hours later, they destroyed all the Jordanian air force and half of Syria's on the ground.[17]

These overwhelmingly successful surprise attacks guaranteed an Israeli victory before the ground war could get started.

After just six days of fighting, the Israeli forces on the ground had captured the Sinai, the Gaza Strip, the West Bank and the Golan Heights. Most important, they were able to conquer the Old City of Jerusalem and regain control of the sacred Temple Mount.

After breaking into the Old City, the Israeli troops rushed to the Western Wall of the Temple Mount to pray. No Jew had been allowed access to that area for 18 years, ever since the Jordanians had taken the city in the War of Independence. Rabbi Shlomo Goren, the chief rabbi of the Israel army (and later the chief rabbi of Israel) rushed to the wall. He had a torah scroll under one arm and a shofar in the other hand. He blew the shofar and announced: "We have taken the City of God. We are entering the Messianic era for the Jewish people."[18]

He said that because he knew from prophecies in the Hebrew scriptures that when the Jews are back in the land and back in their capital city, the Messiah will come.

Once again, the tiny nation of Israel had prevailed against unbeatable odds, just as prophesied in the ancient Hebrew scriptures. The victory had been achieved with lightning swiftness, in only six days, proving to be one of the most miraculous wars in history.

C. The Yom Kippur War (October 1973)

The situation proved to be quite different in 1973 when the Arabs enjoyed the element of surprise. Egypt and Syria launched an all-out surprise attack against Israel on October 6, which happened to be Yom Kippur, the holiest day in Judaism.

The Egyptians suddenly crossed the Suez Canal, quickly overran the Israeli outposts along the canal, and then drove deep into the Sinai before the Israelis could mobilize their forces, deploy them, and launch a counter-attack. Meanwhile, the Syrians had simultaneously attacked the Golan Heights.

The war was prompted by a desire on the part of the Egyptian President, Anwar Sadat, to avenge the humiliation the Arab world had suffered in the 1967 Six Day War. Although Sadat warned repeatedly in 1971, 1972 and 1973 that he was going to renew the war with Israel, most observers remained skeptical.

CHAPTER NINE

It was not until a few hours before the attack began that the Israeli Chief of Staff, David Elazar, recommended a full, immediate mobilization and a preemptive air strike. But he was overruled by Prime Minister Golda Meir who feared that striking first would anger the United States and motivate President Nixon to refuse to support Israel.[19]

The news of the attack also caught the U.S. by surprise because the very day before, the CIA had reported to President Nixon "that war in the Middle East is unlikely."[20]

Once again, as in all its previous wars, Israel faced overwhelming odds.

On the Golan Heights, approximately 180 Israeli tanks faced an onslaught of 1,400 Syrian tanks. Along the Suez Canal, fewer than 500 Israeli defenders with only 3 tanks were attacked by 600,000 Egyptian soldiers, backed by 2,000 tanks and 550 aircraft.

Furthermore, at least nine Arab states provided aid to the Egyptian-Syrian war effort, including Saudi Arabia and Kuwait who served as the financial underwriters. Most important, the Soviet Union was heavily involved, providing military supplies, intelligence and diplomatic support.[21]

Israel prevailed because of massive aid from the Nixon Administration and because of brilliant generalship in the marshalling of its armies.

The U.S. supplied $2.2 billion in emergency aid that totaled 22,000 tons of equipment that was transported to Israel in 566 flights.[22]

The Israeli military leaders utilized this aid to stop the Syrians dead in their tracks on the Golan Heights, while General Ariel Sharon led the Israeli tank forces in the Sinai in a counterattack that resulted in the greatest tank battle in history.

IS THE END NEAR???

By October 15, the Egyptian tank force had been destroyed, and Sharon had crossed the Suez Canal. He quickly surrounded the Egyptian Third Army, immobilized it, and started marching toward Cairo.

Meanwhile, in the north, the Israeli forces had cleared the Golan Heights, recaptured Mount Hermon and started driving toward Damascus.

Israeli forces were 25 miles from Damascus and 63 miles from Cairo when the Soviets decided to pressure the United Nations into calling for a cease fire.

Once again, Israel had prevailed when there seemed to be no hope.

D. <u>Operation Thunderbolt</u> (July 1976)

On June 27, 1976, an Air France flight from Tel Aviv to Paris made a stopover in Athens where it unloaded some passengers and picked up others. Among those who got on the flight were four terrorists, two Palestinians and two Germans. They hijacked the flight as soon as it took off, and they then diverted it to Benghazi, Libya where it was refueled. From there they headed to Entebbe, Uganda, where the President of the country, Idi Amin, was waiting to welcome them.[23]

Upon landing, four more terrorists joined the group, and they proceeded to separate the hostages.

All the Jews were herded into a recently abandoned terminal building. The rest of the passengers were released and flown to Paris. The Air France crew decided to stay behind with the Jewish hostages. The number of hostages, including the crew, totaled 106.

CHAPTER NINE

The hijackers immediately issued an ultimatum: Either release 53 terrorists held in Israel and four in other countries, or all the hostages would be killed on July 1. The Israeli government launched negotiations with the terrorists while considering a military alternative. As a result of the negotiations, the hijackers agreed to extend the deadline to July 4.

A military alternative was considered by most to be unthinkable, mainly because of the great distance involved — 2,500 miles from Tel Aviv to Entebbe. Nonetheless, the Israeli Cabinet ordered the preparation of a rescue mission while they used the negotiations to stall for time.

As it turned out, the Israelis had two advantages working for them. They were able to interview all the passengers who had been released, and from them they got detailed information about the captors and the hostages. They also discovered that the abandoned terminal building had been built by an Israeli company, so they were able to get the blueprints of the building!

Lieutenant Colonel Jonathan (Yoni) Netanyahu was selected to lead the commando assault team. He was the older brother of the man who would later become the prime minister of Israel — Benjamin Netanyahu.

Although Yoni was only 30 years old, he had accumulated an outstanding record of military leadership and daring. To prepare his team for the attack, he came up with the idea of using hay bales to lay out the exact floor plan of the terminal building, and his commando team began practicing mock assaults.

IS THE END NEAR???

Four Lockheed C-130 Hercules aircraft, plus two Boeing 747s were used in the raid. More than 100 personnel were recruited and divided into teams. Yoni's assault group consisted of 29 elite commandos. A second group was assigned the job of encircling the new terminal building and immobilizing the Ugandan soldiers attached to it. A further group was given the task of destroying all the MiG fighter planes on the ground at the airport. A fourth group was given the task of refueling the airplanes, and a fifth squad was put in charge of evacuating the hostages.

The mission was launched on the afternoon of July 3. The planes flew most of the way at an altitude of only 100 feet in order to avoid radar detection. The flight took 7 hours and 40 minutes.

They arrived one minute behind schedule at 11:01pm Israeli time — but just after midnight in Uganda, the beginning of July 4, 1976. The surprise blitz attack proved successful beyond any expectations. It took a total of only 53 minutes.

During that time, all seven of the hijackers who were present were killed, together with 33 to 45 Ugandan soldiers, and all 8 MIG fighter planes on the ground were destroyed.[24]

Three hostages died in the crossfire, and ten were wounded. One was left behind because she had been taken to a hospital in Entebbe. A total of 102 hostages were taken back to Israel alive.[25]

Five Israeli commandos were wounded. Only one was killed — the leader of the raid, Yoni Netanyahu.

CHAPTER NINE

The entire raid, including the refueling of the planes and the evacuation of the hostages, took a total of only one hour and 39 minutes.[26]

To this day, this amazing raid is considered to be one of the most outstanding examples of military planning, coordination and execution in the annals of military history.

E. **Operation Opera (June 1981)**

In 1976 Iraq purchase an "Osiris-class" nuclear reactor from France. The site chosen for the reactor was about 10 miles southeast of Baghdad. It was given the name of Osirak.

While both France and Iraq claimed that the Osirak reactor was for peaceful scientific research, the Israelis viewed the whole project with great suspicion. When both American and Israeli intelligence sources confirmed Iraq's intention to use the reactor to develop nuclear weapons, the Israelis launched an intensive diplomatic effort to try to halt the French financial and scientific support for the project, but all diplomatic efforts failed.[27]

In early 1981 when the Israeli Cabinet received word that a shipment of 90 kilograms of enriched uranium fuel rods was expected to be supplied by France any moment, they decided to prepare for an immediate attack.[28] This decision was, of course, prompted by a desire to prevent the reactor from being activated. But it was also motivated by a concern that if the attack occurred after activation, it would pose a radiation threat to the inhabitants of Baghdad.[29]

IS THE END NEAR???

The mission to destroy the Osirak reactor was launched on June 7, 1981. The attack squadron consisted of eight F-16s, each with two 2,000 pound bombs, and six F-15s, which were assigned the task of providing fighter support.[30]

The planes flew low over Saudi Arabia to avoid radar detection. They caught the Iraqis by complete surprise and completely destroyed the reactor in an attack that took less than two minutes. All the Israeli planes returned home safely.

In a weird coincidence, King Hussein of Jordan was vacationing on his yacht in the Gulf of Aqaba at the time. Since the Israeli jets took off from the Etzion Airbase in the southern Negev desert, they flew directly over the King's yacht, and when he saw them, he immediately jumped to the conclusion that they were headed to Iraq to bomb the Osirak reactor. He called his office in Amman and asked them to send an urgent warning to Iraq, but for some unknown reason, the warning was never received by the Iraqis.[31]

Also, it was learned after the attack that half an hour before the Israeli planes arrived, the group of Iraqi soldiers manning the anti-aircraft defenses for the reactor had left their posts for an afternoon meal, and they had turned off their radar detectors.[32]

The leader of the attack force, Ze'ev Raz, was interviewed in 2007 by the Jewish Press. As he was recounting the events, the interviewer said, "The way you are describing it, it sounds like an outright miracle." Raz responded, "Absolutely. Of course it was a miracle. How is it possible that even after we bombed the reactor not one plane tried to down us?" He then continued with an amazing observation:[33]

CHAPTER NINE

I'll tell you something else: It takes an hour and a half to get back from Iraq to Israel and we were flying 40,000 feet above the ground.

The General Staff originally wanted us to carry out the bombing after sunset so it would be harder for the Iraqis to attack us on the way back. But I was opposed to that. I thought if we did the bombing after sunset there wouldn't be enough light and our planes would miss their target — so I insisted that the bombing take place before sunset.

As a result, we flew back as the sun was setting. But since the planes were traveling [so high and] at such a fast speed, the sun was out all the time and never set. It was as though it remained standing in the middle of the horizon.

At that time we pilots all radioed each other reciting the same exact biblical verse — Joshua 10:12: "Sun, stand still over Gibeon, and moon, over the Valley of Ayalon."

I am convinced that the examples cited above prove beyond a doubt that God has His hand on Israel, protecting the Jewish people from assault after assault, and enabling them to achieve miraculous victories — all in fulfillment of Bible prophecies about Israel in the end times.

Nor can there be any doubt that God's supernatural protection will continue for the immediate future (**Psalm 121:4**).

Currently, a major war looms over the Middle East as Arab secular leaders are being replaced by Muslim fundamentalists who are determined to "liberate" Jerusalem and annihilate Israel.

IS THE END NEAR???

It could well prove to be the worst of all the wars Israel has experienced because missiles are going to rain down on the nation from all directions.

But if Psalm 83 is a prophecy about this war, as I think it could well be, then Israel will once again be overwhelmingly victorious, defeating all the Arab nations with whom it shares a common border. This will pave the way for the subsequent war of Gog and Magog, described in Ezekiel 38 and 39, when Russia, accompanied by certain Muslim nations, will come down against Israel and will suffer supernatural destruction at the hands of the Lord.

Israel has some very difficult days ahead, but God has made some wonderful promises to them that they can rely on. In **Psalm 121:4** He says, **"Behold, He who keeps Israel will neither slumber nor sleep."** In **Isaiah 54:17** He promises, **"No weapon formed against you shall prosper."** And in **Joel 3:2** He states that He will severely judge all nations in the end times who get involved in trying to divide up **"My land."**

Another of God's powerful promises to Israel is found in **Isaiah 41:8-16.**

Our nation needs to pay attention to these promises of God. In recent years, we have put enormous pressure on Israel to follow a path of appeasement by "trading land for peace." In the process we have increasingly given encouragement to Israel's sworn enemies. If we continue to manhandle Israel, we will end up guaranteeing our own destruction.

With all this said, and it is a lot, **AMEN!**

CHAPTER NINE

Let me finalize this message with:

The Jews in End Time Bible Prophecy

As you can see with what we have covered in detail, I believe that we are living in exciting times when we can witness Bible prophecy being fulfilled before our very eyes. Many of these prophecies relate to the Jewish people and their nation.

In conclusion let me give you a quick summary of prophecies concerning the Jews that are currently being fulfilled and those that are yet to be fulfilled.

1. **Prophecies Currently Being Fulfilled**

    A. The Jewish people will be regathered in **unbelief** from the four corners of the earth **(Isaiah 11:11-12)**. **Fulfillment**: **21st Century and continuing**.

    B. The state of Israel will be re-established (**Isaiah 66:7-8 and Ezekiel 37:21-22**). **Fulfillment**: May 14, 1948.

    C. The Jews will once again re-occupy the city of Jerusalem (**Zechariah 8:4-8**), **Fulfillment**: June 7, 1967.

    D. The land of Israel will be reclaimed from its desolation, becoming once again a land of agricultural abundance (**Ezekiel 36:34-35**). **Fulfillment: 20th Century and continuing**.

    E. The Hebrew language will be revived from the dead (**Zephaniah 3:9**). Fulfillment: 19th & 20th Centuries.

    F. All the nations of the world will come together against Israel over the issue of the control of Jerusalem (**Zechariah 12:1-3**). **Fulfillment: Currently occurring**.

IS THE END NEAR???

2. **Prophecies Yet To Be Fulfilled**

   A. The **Arab nations** of the world will attack Israel in a coordinated effort to annihilate the state (**Psalm 83**).

   B. Israel will soundly defeat the Arab **alliance** (**Zechariah 12:6**).

   C. Israel will dwell in **security and prosperity** (**Ezekiel 38:11**).

   D. A Russian coalition consisting mainly of Muslim nations will invade Israel (**Ezekiel 38:1-17**).

   E. The **Russian** coalition will be destroyed supernaturally by God (**Ezekiel 38:18-23 and 39:1-8**).

   F. The **Antichrist** will intervene and guarantee the security of Israel, enabling the Jews to rebuild their Temple (**Daniel 9:27**).

   G. At the end of three and a half years, the Antichrist will enter the rebuilt Temple in Jerusalem and **declare** himself to be God (**Daniel 9:27, Matthew 24:15-18**, and **2 Thessalonians 2:3-4**).

   H. The Jews will reject the Antichrist, and he will respond with an attempt to **annihilate** them, killing two-thirds of them in the process (**Revelation 12:13-17** and **Zechariah 13:8-9**).

   I. At the end of the Tribulation, when the Jews have come to the end of themselves, they will **turn** to God and receive Yeshua as their Messiah (**Zechariah 12:10, Romans 9:27-28**, and **Romans 11:25-27**).

   J. Jesus will return and regather all **believing** Jews to Israel (**Deuteronomy 30:1-9**).

CHAPTER NINE

K. Israel will be established as the **prime** nation in the world (**Isaiah 2:1-4** and **Micah 4:1-7**).

L. The Lord will bless the Jewish remnant by **fulfilling** all the promises He has made to Israel (**Isaiah 60:1-62:7**).

M. The blessings of God will flow out to all the nations through the Jewish people during the **Millennial** rule of Jesus (**Zechariah 8:22-23**).

3. **Prophecies Concerning the Church**.

   Christians should find the fulfillment of these prophecies very encouraging because God has also made a lot of promises through Bible prophecy to the Church. As we see the Lord fulfilling every promise He has made to the Jews, we can be assured that He will fulfill all the promises He has made to the Church through His Prophetic Word.

   He has promised that one day very soon, His Son will appear in the Heavens. There will be the shout of an archangel and the blowing of a shofar, and all the dead in Christ will be resurrected to meet Him in the sky. And those of us who are alive will be taken up also, not even experiencing death (**1 Thessalonians 4:13-18**). We will receive glorified, perfected bodies (**Isaiah 35:5-6** and **Philippians 3:21**). We will return to Heaven with the Lord to await the end of the Tribulation (**John 14:1-4**).

   While in Heaven, we will be judged to receive our degrees of rewards (**2 Corinthians 5:10**) and we will celebrate our union with the Lord at the "Marriage Supper of the Lamb" (**Revelation 19:7-9**).

IS THE END NEAR???

We will then return with the Lord to this earth **(Revelation 19:14)**, and we will reign with Him for a thousand years **(Revelation 20:1-6)**. During that glorious reign, we will see the earth flooded with peace, righteousness and justice, as the waters cover the seas **(Isaiah 11:1-9)**.

At the end of the Millennium, we will be removed from this earth to the New Jerusalem the Lord has been preparing for us, and from that vantage point, we will witness the greatest fireworks display in history as God envelops this earth in fire, burning away the pollution of Satan's last revolt **(2 Peter 3:10-13)**. Out of that fiery inferno will come new heavens and a new earth where we will live forever in the New Jerusalem in the presence of Almighty God and His Son **(Revelation 21:1-7)**.

Maranatha!

Come Quickly,

Lord Jesus!

CHAPTER NINE

THOUGHTS:

_____

_____

_____

_____

_____

ACTIONS:

_____

_____

_____

_____

_____

_____

CHAPTER TEN

REVELATION OF THE MAN OF SIN

OR

SATAN'S SUPERMAN

CHAPTER TEN

II Thessalonians 2:1-10

I heard of a man who always wanted a barometer. So he ordered one, a very expensive model from a well known company, minutely calibrated to tell the weather. He wanted to set it somewhere in his house, perhaps on the mantle so he carefully unpacked it and he looked at it and the needle was pointed to the sector that says hurricane. Well he shook it and it still didn't adjust. He shook it again but the needle just stayed that way. He then said, "As much as I paid for this thing and it is defective!" He lived on Long Island and on his way to the city, he wrote a scorching letter to this company for sending him a defective barometer. When he arrived back at Long Island, the barometer was gone and so was his house, because that was in 1938 and the great hurricane had come through.

You see there was nothing wrong with the barometer, he just refused to believe it that a hurricane was coming.

I give you this story to tell you there is nothing wrong with the Word of God and <u>it does not need any adjustment</u>---**<u>IT JUST NEEDS BELIEVING</u>!!!!!!!**

IS THE END NEAR???

In our text God is telling us that there are storms coming to this old world and it warns of this coming destruction, the worst ever in mankind's history, called **THE GREAT TRIBULATION!**

In our text, 2 Thessalonians 2:1-12, it tells us of the rise of a man called, IN THE BIBLE, the man of sin. Who is this man????

I would like to call him **SATAN'S SUPERMAN!**

Now let me say this, I believe, along with many other great preachers, not than I am one of these, but I believe as they do, that this man is standing already in the wings of time, a man who will be the devil incarnate. He will be Satan in human form and he is called the beast. He is called the antichrist. He is called the man of sin. He is called the son of perdition and our text warns us about this one and we had better not be ignorant or bland to his existence!

Now let me give you the background of the verses that I've just read to you. The Apostle Paul says that Christ is coming, but then in verse two he says,

"Don't be shaken in mind or troubled" Now why were these people shaken? Why were they troubled?

Well a bogus letter had gone out, in other words, **a forged letter**, somebody had signed Paul's name to it and told these people they were already in the great tribulation. The day of the Lord had come.

Notice verse two, Paul says, "that you be not soon shaken in mind or be troubled, neither by spirit, nor by word, nor by letter as from us."

CHAPTER TEN

That is some bogus letter that pretends to be from us, that the day of Christ is at hand.

Now remember, the day of Christ, this may literally be translated the day of the Lord, the tribulation is already here. And there were some who were feeling that they were already in the day of the Lord. That dark day that I was telling you about, the last time we met, **that great tribulation**. Remember that they, those that had died, had missed the rapture and that they had gone in to the tribulation and the Apostle Paul is using the occasion of a lie **to tell the truth**.

That's what I want to do---I want to use this opportunity to tell you the truth concerning the second coming of Jesus Christ and those things that are about to transpire. Now then as we looked at this passage--I want to give you six thoughts and want you to look at them, very carefully, with me.

The <u>mockery</u> of God is <u>recounted</u>. Look at verse three, chapter 2:3-5 Folks there is coming and has already come, an awful mockery of God!

- ❖ Apparently, mocking Jesus has become the order of the day in our society. Lady Gaga is one of the biggest offenders, yet people still purchase her music. She recorded a song call "Judas" in which she says she's in love with the betrayer of Jesus. Is it worth compromising your soul to listen to that?

- ❖ Gay groups in San Francisco held a "Hunky Jesus" contest recently, complete with crosses, men with beards and crowns of thorns. And, of course, we shouldn't call them out on that because if we do, we're not "loving them" as Jesus would.

IS THE END NEAR???

While Jesus would continue to love them and pray for them, as we all should as Christians, **there is going to come a time when God is going to get fed up with all of this, and Christians' indifference to these incidents.**

I shouldn't have to remind everyone that Jesus did get angry, especially in the temple when he drove out the moneychangers and said, "It is written, 'My house shall be called a house of prayer, but you have made it a den of thieves.'" (Matthew 21:13).

So Paul recounts this mockery of God that is to come. Now what Paul is saying is this that Satan is going to fling one final insult into the face of heaven's king. And the agent of this blasphemy, the agent of this insult to the Almighty is going to be what the Bible calls the man of sin.

Notice verse three, *"that day shall not come except there comes a falling away first and that that man of sin be revealed."* Now when the Bible uses the term, the man of sin, it is the many aliases in the Bible for the anti-christ.

As a matter of fact, you can read this passage through in about five or six different translations. Some call the man of sin, **the man of lawlessness**. Another translation called the man of sin, **the incarnation of wickedness**. Another translation called the man of sin, **the champion of wickedness**. Another translation called the man of sin, **wickedness in human form**. The man of sin, **the epitome of evil, the distillation of the demonic**.

All of these are terms that describe this character who is about to appear on the stage of human life, the man of sin. The man of sin

CHAPTER TEN

speaks of his character. He's also called the son of perdition in this same verse, the son of perdition. The word, perdition means **judgment**. And he is destined for divine destruction.

He is going to be the devil in human form. He will be the devil incarnate.

Satan is always God's imitator. Martin Luther called him God's ape, meaning by that that he imitates God. Satan's burning ambition has always been, I will be like the most high. So if God has his Christ, Satan has his Antichrist. Now "anti", the prefix anti, and **by the way the Apostle John is the only one in the Bible who uses the term Antichrist**, and he uses it over and over again.

Anti means two things, the prefix. **Number one it means against**, but **number two it means instead of**. And that's exactly what the beast is. He is against Christ, but he also presents himself instead of Christ. The devil has always wanted to be worshipped. And as Jesus Christ is to the Father, the Antichrist is to the devil.

Jesus could say, when He was here on earth, he that has seen me, has seen my Father. The Antichrist, would be able to say, he who has seen me, has seen my father, only his father is the devil, as you will see. He will be Satan in human flesh.

You see, the devil has always wanted the undiluted and undisguised worship of men.

So notice what he is going to do. In verse four, *"he's one who opposes and exalts himself above all that is called God, or that is worshipped; so that he as God sitteth in the temple of God, shewing himself that he is God."*

IS THE END NEAR???

Now learn this about the devil, he doesn't want casualties, **he wants converts**. The devil wants worship so that he as God sitteth in the temple of God showing himself that he is God.

With burning eloquence and ambition, the devil had said in Isaiah chapter fourteen, I will be like the most high. He's always wanted to be worshipped.

He's going to receive that worship through this one that the bible calls the man of sin, the son of perdition. It's very interesting.

Notice Verse four says **"he's going to sit in the temple of God, showing himself that he is God".** Well you say, pastor how can he do that?

There is no temple. The temple was destroyed, in 70 A.D. You're correct, but the temple will be rebuilt. You say do you believe that? Yes I do. I believe that the temple is going to be rebuilt shortly after the rapture of the church.

There will be a three and a half year period when the Antichrist will hold sway. He will make a league with the nation Israel and he will put all of the resources of the world into building there, for the Jewish people, a magnificent temple. You say, do they want a temple?

Of course they do. In some Rabbinacle circles the question is being considered already, whether the time has come to erect a temple in Jerusalem. Let me give you a recent quotation from Israel. The Israeli Press says, and I quote, *"In the ministry of religion a document concerning this was put forward in which proposals from all of the world were collected. Religious activists are for the erection of the temple as soon as possible. There's some opposition, but everything urges toward the building of the temple."* And in a recent ceremony Israel's Minister of Religion, Abner Shakey, saw a

CHAPTER TEN

model of the seven branch temple candelabra. An artist Shiam Odem, who is an immigrant from the Soviet Union, designed that candelabra that will go in this temple. And the only thing that's kept them from building it, or one of the things that has kept them from building it, it takes ninety-five pounds of gold.

One American businessman, Morris Prague, has already pledged one hundred thousand dollars to build this seven prong candlestick for the temple.

Here's a report that comes from Jerusalem, "Rabbi Yishrael Areal, cautiously opens the door to a special treasury, located in the old city, with a number of keys. This is the entrance to a study and research facility for temple equipment. To the question, is it time to build the temple? The rabbi answers, 'Ezra and Nehemiah did not wait for a temple to come down from heaven, but they laid on hands to make it a reality'. Yishrael Areal and his associates have already created some remarkable works, among which are silver trumpets, priests' robes, a wash basin, a harp and even a box for casting lots to select the scapegoat. Everything is done precisely and in accordance with scripture instructions." So one of these days the temple will be rebuilt.

And the Antichrist may even now be standing in the wings.

Look if you will, in verse three, **"Let no man deceive you by any mean for that day shall not come except there comes a falling away first and the man of sin revealed."** Do you see the word revealed? Now he can be present and not be revealed. The word revealed is the Apocalypse's, it's the word we get apocalypse from and it literally means an unveiling. Perhaps some character, some person alive today is that one who will step on to the stage and will become what is known as the beast, the anti-christ, the son of perdition. But I just simply want to say that Paul recounts the mockery of God.

There's coming one who will sit in the temple of God showing himself that he is God.

Not only is the mockery of God recounted, but the <u>mystery</u> of iniquity is <u>restrained</u>. Now look in verse six, ***"and now ye know what withholdeth that he might be revealed in his time."*** Now there is something that is holding back, restraining this Antichrist.

Notice in verse seven, ***"for the mystery of iniquity doth already work: only he who now letteth will let, until he be taken out of the way."***

Now the word "letteth" in the King James Version of the scripture means restrained. So he's saying the mystery of iniquity is already at work. The mystery of iniquity was at work in Paul's time. And the word, work, means to work with power. What the Apostle Paul is saying is there is a force, a wicked, malevolent force that I am calling the mystery of iniquity. It is that force that will energize the Antichrist. He said, it is at work in my time. Certainly you and I are seeing the works of the Antichrist today. Those works are restrained. That is it's as if the devil is on a leash. But this devilish conspiracy, the Bible calls the mystery of iniquity. **Now what is the mystery of iniquity?**

Well the mystery of iniquity is a plot hatched in hell. It is a devilish conspiracy against the human race by an unseen spirit world.

May I tell you there are spirit beings that the Bible calls demons? They are organized, they are brilliant, they are invisible, they are powerful and they are tireless. Well you say, I don't believe in demons.

CHAPTER TEN

May I remind you that medieval doctors didn't believe in bacteria, but they were harmed by them. And the Bible says in **Ephesians 6:12 (KJV)**, *"for we wrestle not against flesh and blood, but against principalities, against powers, against the rulers of the darkness of this world, against spiritual wickedness in high places."* There is a mystery of iniquity. But the Bible teaches that it is restrained, that it's being held back.

Now the mockery of God is recounted, but the mystery of iniquity is restrained. There is something, someone, somehow keeping anti-christ from doing what he wants to do. So we now move to:

1. **The ministry of the spirit will be <u>removed</u>!!!! Now notice II Thessalonians 2:7-8,**

"For the mystery of iniquity doth already work: only he who now let's," that is he who now restrains, *"will restrain until he be taken out of the way."* Now notice the word, <u>he</u>, and just <u>put a circle around he</u>.

"Then shall that Wicked," **notice the word <u>wicked</u> is capitalized**, it means wicked one, then shall that Wicked one *"be revealed, whom the Lord shall destroy with the spirit of his mouth, and shall destroy with the brightness of his coming:"*

Now go back to chapter two, verse six, *"and ye know what withholdeth,"* now put a circle around the word **WHAT**. And then in verse seven, you have a circle around the word he.

There is a **"WHAT"** who is restraining the man of sin and there is a **"HE"** who is restraining the man of sin.

IS THE END NEAR???

Now there is someone and something that is holding back the Antichrist. Now if you look at verse 6-7...did you notice that we find that verse six speaks of the church and verse seven speaks of the Holy Spirit.

Where does the Holy Spirit abide?

- ❖ He lives in us.
- ❖ He resides in us, the church of the Lord Jesus Christ.

In verse six the **"HE"** is the Holy Spirit who lives in the **"WHAT"**? **The Holy Spirit lives in me and everyone that has received Christ as their personal Savior, i.e. BORN AGAIN!**

Now then, as long as the church is here, then **the Antichrist cannot have full sway**, because when the Antichrist comes, God is going to pour out his wrath upon this world, but you see my friend, God has not appointed us to wrath. **And the church is here restraining the power of Antichrist.**

You see, the church is the salt of the earth. **What does salt do?** Well, my friend, salt cleanses, salt purifies, salt flavors, salt penetrates, salt preserves. **When the salt is taken out, the corruption will begin. The Holy Spirit of God is in the church.**

Now the Holy Spirit, He has two ministries. Ministry number <u>one</u> is to help the saints, ministry number <u>two</u> is to hinder Satan. There's only so far that Satan can go and God allows Satan to have power but not all power. Even when Satan wanted to harm Job, God said, there's only so far that you can go.

CHAPTER TEN

Christian let me tell you that Satan is on a leash. But my dear friend, the ministry of the spirit is going to be removed! **At the rapture of the church, when the church is taken out, the Holy Spirit's influence through the church will be removed from this earth.**

Now listen closely: That doesn't mean the Holy Spirit will not be here, there's no place where the spirit is not. The Bible says, *"if I make my bed in hell, oh thou art there."*

God is everywhere!!! What he is talking about is the power of the Holy Spirit manifest through the church is going to be taken out.

The "WHAT" in <u>verse six</u> is the church, the **"WHO"** in <u>verse seven is the Holy Spirit taken out at the church</u>.

Notice how Paul began this thing, chapter two…. "Now we beseech you therefore brethren by the coming of our Lord Jesus Christ, by our gathering together unto him." When he comes, the dead in Christ shall rise first and we which remain and are alive will be caught up to meet the Lord in the air. And when we are taken out, the Holy Spirit stands aside and then this mystery of iniquity that has been restrained will be restrained no more. And when that happens dear friend, to stop the flood tide of filth and iniquity and cruelty, a horror will be impossible.

Aderin Rogers said, *"You might as well try to dam up Niagara Falls with toothpicks as to stop the flood of wickedness that will come to this world."* So that brings me to the second thing.

    2.   The <u>mastery</u> of Satan is <u>released</u>. Let's read
        II Thessalonians 2:7-11. What a terrifying passage this is.

IS THE END NEAR???

Now remember this, the man of sin is going to be Satan incarnate. He is going to receive power from the devil himself. Let's look back again----verse nine, ***"Even him, whose coming is after the working of Satan with all power and signs and lying wonders."***

What will this Antichrist be like? I've called him the Satan's Superman.

- His intellectual genius will be immense.
- His authority, overpowering.
- His hatreds, extraordinary.
- His techniques, superb.
- Men will be willing to die for him and women will swoon at his feet.
- Little children will speak his name with reverence.

The Bible says, the entire world will marvel, will wonder at the beast.

When I use the word "**BEAST**," don't get the idea of someone who is ferocious outwardly, who is repulsive outwardly!

Oh no, this speaks of his <u>**character**</u>, not his appearance.

You see, the beast is the second person in the unholy trinity. **God has a holy trinity, Father, Son and Holy Spirit.**

The devil has an unholy trinity, the dragon, <u>**the beast and the false prophet**</u>.

- The dragon is Satan,
- the beast is the Antichrist,

CHAPTER TEN

- ❖ the false prophet is the sinister, minister of propaganda who will cause people to worship the beast as the Holy Spirit causes people to worship the Lord Jesus Christ.

Now this lawless one is going to ride into power on a platform of fame and fortune and the biggest plank in his platform is going to be world peace.

NOW - - In **Daniel 8: 23-25** and just let me read these verses to you------now---when Daniel said:

- ❖ *"and in the latter time of their kingdom,"* he's talking about certain kings,

- ❖ *"when the transgressors are come to the full, a king of fierce countenance, and understanding dark sentences, shall stand up."* Fierce countenance that means no one can stand against him. Understanding dark sentences means that he has probed the occult.

- ❖ And verse twenty-four, *"and his power shall be mighty, but not by his own power:"*

- ❖ that is, Satan's Superman is receiving power from the devil: *"and he shall destroy wonderfully, and shall prosper, and practice, and shall destroy the mighty and the holy people."*

- ❖ <u>The holy people are the Jews</u>. *"And through his policy also he shall cause craft to prosper in his hand; and he shall magnify himself in his heart,"* and

IS THE END NEAR???

listen to this next phrase, *"and by peace shall destroy many,"* by peace. That is he will come as an imitation of the Prince of Peace. He will make a peace treaty with Israel. At last Israel will say "Our Messiah has come."

- ❖ Jesus knew they would do this. **John 5:43,** Jesus said, **"I have come in my Father's name, and ye receive me not: if another shall come in his own name, him ye shall receive."**

- ❖ This coming devil's messiah will come out of the unified Europe that we are seeing take form right now before our eyes. He will make a peace treaty with Israel, He will help them to rebuild their temple, but as soon as it's rebuilt, **he will move into that temple and say**, *"you want to worship God, well you're looking at him am God."* And at that time, this one who has done such lying wonders will turn on God's ancient people with unspeakable wrath.

That dear Christian is what the **Bible calls the time of Jacob's trouble-Jeremiah 30:7**. It's the time that Jesus warned about when he said, *"for then shall be great tribulation."*

You see, the devil has power. He has power to work miracles. Look again in verse nine. **"Even him, whose coming is after the working of Satan with all power and signs and lying wonders"** (II Thessalonians 2:9 KJV).

Those that are living may say, I wouldn't believe his lie. My friend, I'll promise those that have not trusted Christ, you'll believe his lies if you go into the great tribulation after having heard the gospel of Jesus Christ and refusing it.

CHAPTER TEN

"For this cause God shall send them strong delusion," the Bible says, *"that they should believe the lie, because they received not the love of the truth that they might be saved."* Some may say, "I didn't think the devil had power to work miracles."

Revelation 16:13-14, "and I saw three unclean spirits like frogs come out of the mouth of the *dragon*," (that's the anti-God), **"and out of the beast,"** (that's the Antichrist), **"out of the mouth of the false prophet"** (that's the anti-spirit). **"For they are the spirits of devils, working miracles, which go forth unto the kings of the earth and of the whole world, to gether them to the battle of that great day of God Almighty."**

- ❖ What I'm trying to say--is my dear friend, there's coming a time when Hell will have a holiday.

- ❖ **There is coming a time when the church is taken out, the Holy Spirit stands back, the leash is removed and Satan's mastery is released. And Satan will have his way on this world and he will rule through his vice regent, the man of sin, the son of perdition.**

3. I want you to notice, the <u>misery of man is redoubled</u>. Look, if you will now in 2 Thessalonians 2:11-12……… *"for this cause."*

God shall send "**THEM**," who? The people on earth, *"strong delusion that they should believe a lie: That they all might be damned who believed not the truth."*

IS THE END NEAR???

They sat in a church like this and heard a preacher tear his heart out and beg people to be saved, but oh no, they wanted their own selfish, sinful way, they receive not the love of the truth, but had pleasure in unrighteousness. They wanted their own sins.

And the Bible says, *"that they all might be damned who believe not the truth, but had pleasure in unrighteousness."*

The **misery** of man is redoubled. Antichrist, when he comes, is going to turn this entire world into a vast concentration camp with all of the inmates numbered.

What will he be like? He will be the Caesars, the Napoleons, the Hitler's, the Stalin's, the Khomeini's, the Saddam Husseins, the Putins--- all melted into one person and how he will regiment everyone.

We're going to speak later perhaps, in concluding this series about the mark of the beast. BUT FOR NOW - we all know how much man relies on the computers and these instruments will help him regiment everyone. Already we're being regimented. Now these people have gone beyond the normal credit card we use and not those smart cards that have computer chips (which I told you some time back in 2008 in a series in Revelation) in your card that tells all about you. It would be a very easy thing to take the chip out of the smart card and implant it in a human being. As a matter of fact, all across America right now pets are being taken care of that way. Veterinarians are placing a piece of about the size of a grain of rice in the ear of a pet with a computer chip to help keep up with lost pets, and to help the owners to relocate those pets. You've been given numbers and I've been given numbers.

CHAPTER TEN

You can't get any credit or anything now without your social security number?

Well, when I received mine at the age of 16, I didn't know it was given to me to control me or to identify me. It was simply only a number for the purpose of taking social security taxes out of my paycheck so I could receive a retirement check when I got older!! But now, financial institutions and other companies are using it for identification purposes.

And on some driver licenses in some states, the social security number is on their driver's license.

And now, the IRS is giving a social security number to all little children two years of age, before long, every child will get a number rather than the parent asking for one.

I was reading recently where someone has said, "The way to take care of prisoners today, we can't build enough prisons, but what we can do is to control them with computers." I quote, "in the total control monitoring incorporated system, the prisoners are required to wear an ankle bracelet which accompanies a cellular sending unit. If the prisoner wanders outside a designated radius, the sending unit emits a message to the monitoring device. Operated by brinks who then in turn alerts the correctional authority. The sending unit can be tracked by the monitoring computer and its whereabouts determined at any time company officials indicate it." That just reminds me of something that I read a long time ago, the more machines act like men, the more men will act like machines.

IS THE END NEAR???

LISTEN TO ME FOLKS: WE ARE regimented and the technology is in place and I am telling you dear friend, there is coming a time of terror and the misery of man will be redoubled. Let me come to the last point and this is the glorious part.

Now if you think that I am pessimistic-----you are looking today at a flaming optimist, BECAUSE I want tell you, from the resurrection of Jesus Christ onward, there is not a pessimistic note, not one.

The Apostle Paul is not writing here to threaten these people. He is writing here to comfort these people and to give them hope. And so the last thing----

4. The <u>majesty</u> of Jesus is <u>revealed</u>. When the mastery of Satan is released, that only becomes the black velvet upon which the diamond of His glory will shine all the more.

II Thessalonians 2:8 (KJV)……..WHAT A PROMISE!!!!!!!

"Whom the Lord shall consume with the spirit of His mouth, and shall destroy <u>with the brightness of His coming</u>."

What is the brightness of His coming? **The word brightness here literally means the outshining, the glory, the majesty of His coming.**

Now you need to understand about the second coming of Jesus Christ, while it is one event, **there are two phases to the coming of our Lord Jesus Christ.**

First, he comes for his church and second, he comes with his church. <u>Look, if you will in chapter two, verse one,</u> *"Now we beseech*

CHAPTER TEN

you, brethren, by the coming of our Lord Jesus Christ, and by our gathering together unto him." That's his coming for his church. But now notice in verse eight, *"And then shall that Wicked be revealed, whom the Lord shall consume with the spirit of His mouth, and destroy with the brightness of His coming."* <u>**WATCH THIS NOW**</u>: **That's when our Lord comes with His church. First he comes for his bride, then he comes with his bride**.

This is the reason that some of the people have difficulty understanding the second coming of Jesus and the rapture.

The rapture, dear friend, was a mystery revealed in the New Testament, not taught in the Old Testament.

The Old Testament prophets didn't understand the rapture, they did understand the coming of our Lord in power and glory, but they did not understand the rapture of the church.

And the Apostle Paul says, *"behold I show you a mystery, we shall not all sleep, but we shall all be changed in a moment, in the twinkling of an eye, at the last trump"* (I Corinthians 15:51-52 - KJV). **The rapture is the mystery.**

- ❖ You see, dear friend, there's the mystery of His coming and the majesty of His coming.

- ❖ The mystery of His coming is the rapture.

- ❖ The majesty of His coming is the revelation when he comes in brightness and power and great glory.

IS THE END NEAR???

- ❖ There are many figures of speech. The Lord Jesus is coming suddenly, like the lightening, Matthew 24:27 says, ***"he's coming like a bolt out of the blue."*** The Lord Jesus is coming secretly, like a thief as in I Thessalonians 5:2, which we've already talked about.

- ❖ The Lord Jesus, however, is coming sovereignly as a king, and that's what we're talking about right here in verse eight. My dear friend, Antichrist is going to be destroyed by the brightness of the coming of our Lord and Savior Jesus Christ.

What is going to happen is this, the Antichrist will turn on the Jewish nation after the temple has been rebuilt and he will ensconce himself in the temple of God, showing himself that he is God.

At that time, Israel will realize how betrayed they have been. They are not about to worship any two-legged devil.

At that time, my dear friend, Satan's fury will be poured out **against God's ancient people**. Antichrist, who will have the world's rulers and the world's armies at his disposal, will gather a contingency from all of the armies of the world and have them bibwhacked right there in at Armageddon, the Valley of Jezreel in Edralin. They will be there, army, after army, after army will be there. That place that Napoleon said was the world's greatest natural battlefield.

They will be ready to destroy Israel and finally annihilate, exterminate these dear people that God so dearly loves.

CHAPTER TEN

SJust when the Antichrist, drunk with power is about to make his final move, then heaven will open and Jesus will come, this time not for His saints, but with His saints.

The Bible says the armies that are in heaven will follow Him. And then the Bible says the Lord will destroy him with the spirit of His mouth and the brightness of His coming.

You say, "What is the battle of Armageddon going to be like?" I've told you already, while Antichrist comes with napalm and lasers and atomic warfare and nerve gas and miracles --------**we just have one weapon on our side, it's a sword. And it's in the mouth of our King. The word of God is quick and powerful and sharper than any two edged sword. And He's going to utter two words and the battle will be over and I've told you what they are, "Drop Dead!"**

The Bible says, *"He will slay them with the sword that goeth out of His mouth."* And so ends the career of Antichrist and seven, seven, seven will take care of six, six, six.

And I'm so glad dear friend, that we have the word of God. I'm so glad that we don't have to sit in darkness, but the question comes, are you ready? The question comes, Are you saved? Because if you're not saved and the rapture comes and we're gathered together to meet the Lord Jesus Christ and you're left behind the Bible says, God will send you strong delusion, that you would believe a lie. Antichrist will cause you to betray your mother with a smile on your face. You'll take the brand of the beast and then you'll go into Hell. Satan gives you a number, Jesus gives you a name. And He calls His sheep by name and He's calling you today.

IS THE END NEAR???

THOUGHTS:

ACTIONS:

STUDENT WORKSHEETS

IS THE END NEAR???

CHAPTER ONE

PROPHECY AND THE BOOK OF REVELATION
Introduction to Revelation

I want you to discover the mysteries and wonders revealed in the Book of Revelation of our Lord Jesus Christ as given to the Apostle John.

As we begin the study in the book of Revelation and Prophecy--there are some basic things that we must initially consider.

There are various points of view when it comes to the study of the Book of Revelation. Before we consider the various points of view there are some terms that need to be defined.

1. _____ TERMS:

    a. The _____ Period.
    b. _____.
    c. _____ Tribulation.
    d. _____ Tribulation or _____.
    e. _____.
    f. _____.

2. _____:

    a. The _____ School.
    b. The _____ School.
    c. The _____ School.
    d. The _____ School.

IS THE END NEAR???

3. THEIR _____ - YOUR POINT OF VIEW WILL AFFECT YOU:

    a. _____ or Hermeneutics.
    b. _____ or Immanency.
    c. _____ or _____.

Our Lord's statement to John shows that the Book of Revelation is divided into 3 sections. Let's look at each of them:

1. "Things you have _____."

2. "Things which _____."

3. "Things which shall be _____."

During this study we will devote the next weeks to an in-depth study of the seven major events of Revelation.

1. The Rapture of the Church/_____ of the Saints.

2. The Rise of the Beast/The Devil's _____.

3. The Great Tribulation/Devastation of the _____.

4. _____/Defeat of the Beast and His Armies.

5. The _____ Reign/Peace and Dominion of Jesus. The lamb and lion will lie down together and Jesus will reign (Revelation 20:1-6).

IS THE END NEAR???

6. The Final _____/Doom of _____. "And I saw a great white throne, and Him that sat on it…." (Revelation 20:11-15).

7. The Final State/_____. "And He said unto me, it is done" (Revelation 21:1-22:17).

IS THE END NEAR???

APPLICATION:

ACTION:

IS THE END NEAR???

CHAPTER TWO

THE MYSTERIES AND WONDERS OF PROPHECY
Introduction to Revelation (Continued)

Let's discover the mysteries and wonders revealed in the Revelation of our Lord Jesus Christ as given to the Apostle John.

As we begin the study in the book of Revelation and Prophecy -- there are some basic things that we must initially consider.

There are various points of view when it comes to the study of the book of Revelation. Before we consider the various points of view there are some terms that need to be defined.

1. IMPORTANT TERMS:

    a. The _____ Period.
    b. _____.
    c. _____ Tribulation.
    d. _____ Tribulation or _____.
    e. _____.
    f. _____.

2. COMMON VIEWS:

    a. The _____ School.
    b. The _____ School.
    c. The _____ School.
    d. The _____ School.

IS THE END NEAR???

3. **THEIR IMPLICATIONS – YOUR POINT OF VIEW WILL AFFECT YOU:**

   a. _____ or Hermeneutics.
   b. _____ or Immanency.
   c. _____ or _____.

Our Lord's statement to John shows that the book of Revelation is divided into three sections. Let's look at each of them:

1. "Things you have _____."
2. "Things which _____."
3. "Things which shall be _____."

During this study we will devote the next weeks to an in-depth study of the seven major events of Revelation.

1. The Rapture of the Church/_____ of the Saints.
2. The Rise of the Beast/the Devil's _____.
3. The Great Tribulation/Devastation of the _____.
4. _____ - Defeat of the Beast and His Armies.
5. The _____ Reign/Peace and Dominion of Jesus. The lamb and lion will lie down together and Jesus will reign (Revelation 20:1-6).
6. The Final _____ - Doom of _____. *"And I saw a great white throne, and Him that sat on it...."* (Revelation 20:11-15).
7. The Final State - _____. *"And He said unto me, it is done"* (Revelation 21:1-22:17).

IS THE END NEAR???

APPLICATION:
_____
_____
_____
_____
_____
_____
_____
_____

ACTION:
_____
_____
_____
_____

IS THE END NEAR???

CHAPTER THREE

THE FOUR TERRIBLE HORSEMEN

Revelation 6:1-17

THE FOUR BEASTS: Lion: _____ of Jesus Christ.

Calf: _____ and sacrifice.

Man: _____ of the Lord Jesus Christ.

Eagle: _____.

Seal # 1   White horse: God's _____ on earth.
Crown: "stephanos" meaning the
_____ crown
"diadema" meaning the _____
crown.

Seal # 2   _____ horse _____ or _____.

IS THE END NEAR???

Seal # 3 _____ horse _____.

Seal # 4 _____ horse _____.

FOUR FORMS OF DEATH RELATED TO THIS ATTACK:

The sword—not war but _____.
With murder comes famine and widespread _____.
_____, _____ and _____.
Wild beasts multiply and _____ are subject to attack.

    Seal # 5 _____ under the altar who had been _____ because of the Word of God and the _____ they had maintained.

    Seal # 6 A _____.

IS THE END NEAR???

APPLICATION:

ACTION:

IS THE END NEAR???

CHAPTER FOUR

ANGELS OF DOOM

Revelation 8:1-13

In our studies in the book of Revelation we have been following the unrolling of the seven-sealed scroll which the Lamb of God won the right to open by His death upon the cross. The title of that scroll is "The Mystery of God," and when one reads Chapter 10 we will read in that mystery -- exactly how God is going to bring about universal peace and joy to a sinful, angry, and murderous world -- is completed. God is doing that very thing with individuals even today. Many of you have experienced the peace and joy which God gave you in the midst of the struggles and trials of your life. He does that by grace, by the offer of total forgiveness of sin. But to a world that rejects grace, God can only bring peace through judgment. That is what we are seeing in this book. Six of the seven seals have already been opened when we come to Chapter 8, and we have watched the waves of successive judgments roll across the earth. We learn from the prophet Daniel that these cover a seven-year period in the last days of this age. Under the seals, it is covered from one point of view, i.e., what happens when man is allowed to have his own way. All God does is take away the restraints and let human evil find wider expression. It is limited slightly (to a fourth of the earth), but it finds far greater expression than it does today. That brings us then to the seventh seal which is now opened to us, in Chapter 8:

I.   There is _____ in Heaven.
II.   There is a _____ at the Altar.
III.   There is _____ on Earth.

IS THE END NEAR???

Now let us look at these trumpets and see what they mean.

Angel # 1 sounds his trumpet of _____.

Angel # 2 sounds his trumpet of _____.

Angel # 3 sounds his trumpet of _____.

Angel # 4 sounds his trumpet of _____.

Angel # 5 sounds his trumpet of _____.

    1. They are _____ spirits.

    2. They are _____ spirits (9:2).

    3. They are _____ spirits (9:3-4).

    4. They are _____ spirits (9:5-6).

In these verses we find they were not allowed to kill but to torment for five months.

    5. They are _____ spirits (9:7).

    6. They are _____ spirits (9:7b).

No human ingenuity will be able to stop them.

    7. They are _____ spirits (9:7c).

    8. They are _____ spirits (9:8).

    9. They are _____ spirits (9:9).

    10. They are _____ spirits (9:10).

    11. They are _____ spirits (9:11-12).

IS THE END NEAR???

APPLICATION:

ACTION:

IS THE END NEAR???

CHAPTER FIVE

WHEN ALL "HADES" (HELL) BREAKS LOOSE!

Revelation 9:13-21

The images depicted in this chapter make it one of the most disturbing passages in the entire Bible. In our last session we looked at verses 1-12 where we studied a description of a swarm of demons and the suffering they brought to man.

Now, we come to the Sixth trumpet to sound that a voice is heard to speak between the horns of the golden altar.

I. A TIME OF _____ ACTIVITY:
    Vs. 14 A _____ is mentioned.
    Vs. 15 A _____ is mentioned.
    Vs. 15 A _____ is mentioned.

II. A TIME OF _____ ACTIVITY:
    A. The _____ of this army.
    B. The _____ of this army.

III. A TIME OF _____ ACTIVITY:
    A. Man is _____ in his _____.
    B. Man is _____ in his _____.

IS THE END NEAR???

1. _____.
2. _____.
3. _____.
4. _____.

APPLICATION:

_____

_____

_____

_____

_____

ACTION:

_____

_____

_____

IS THE END NEAR???

CHAPTER SIX

EARTH'S LAST TRIAL

Revelation 15-16

OVERVIEW OF:

CHAPTER 10: The Bitter _____ Book.

CHAPTER 11: The two witnesses: _____.

CHAPTER 12: The woman is _____.

CHAPTER 13: The _____ church.

CHAPTER 14: They represent the resurrected, _____ of God.

CHAPTER 15 and 16 go together describing the _____ last lagues. Verse two gives us three groups in Heaven whom God places in their hands the harps:

    (**1**) those _____ at the second coming of Christ,
    (**2**) those _____ gathered on Mount Zion, and
    (**3**) those that have gone through the _____.

IS THE END NEAR???

CHAPTER 16: We find seven bowls:

1. _____.
2. The bloody _____.
3. The bloody _____.
4. The solar _____.
5. _____.
6. The Euphrates _____.
7. _____ destroyed.

THE BATTLE OF ARMAGEDDON:

1. It is a real geographical site in _____ Israel.
2. God named this as the scene of the _____ battle of this age.
3. The armies that gather at Armageddon will come at the call of _____.
4. The armies of the kings of the _____ will come.
5. The aim is to destroy _____ once and for all.
6. God will appear and rescue Israel and Israel will at last look _____ at Her long awaited Messiah.
7. At this time Christ will come with His _____.
8. Christ will subdue and destroy the forces of _____.

IS THE END NEAR???

APPLICATION:

___

ACTION:

___

IS THE END NEAR???

CHAPTER SEVEN

ONE THOUSAND YEARS OF PEACE

Revelation 20:1-6

The subject for this chapter is about the triumphant and glorious kingdom, the millennial age of our Lord and the **ONE THOUSAND YEARS OF PEACE!!!**

These messages have come and gone so fast that I wish I had more time to preach on this subject. The fullness of the riches of the revelation of God in what He has prepared for His children is immeasurable. It is _____. **It is WONDERFUL** and we have just touched the hem of the garment.

We are going to look at this glorious day that God has promised for His Son and for us in this earth.

Now having given you a small introduction, let me give you five basic things about the **"THOUSAND YEARS OF PEACE or THE GOLDEN AGE"** that will usher in the rule and reign of Jesus Christ on earth.

1. **THE FORCEFUL** _____ of Satan.

2. **THE FUTURE** _____ of the Savior.

    Look at Chapter 20:4-6 ...**WHEN HE RETURNS FOR HIS** millennium reign. Let's look at the _____ that will take place:

        A. The human _____ will change. Turn to Isaiah 2:2-4. . . . .

IS THE END NEAR???

　　B. The _____ kingdom will change.
　　　Isaiah 11:6-9. . . . .

　　C. The _____ and _____ kingdoms will
　　　change. Isaiah 35:1. . . . .

3. The FIRST _____.

What is the first resurrection? Well the Bible gives us the analogy that the first resurrection is like a harvest, which has four general aspects.

　　A. The _____.
　　B. The _____ harvest.
　　C. The _____.
　　D. The _____ with Christ.

4. The _____ **Rebellion of Sinners.**

　Man's _____ is Not the Final Answer.

　　A. _____ is not the answer.
　　B. Changing the _____ is not the answer.

5. THE FIXED _____ OF SIN.

　　A. It provides for us _____.
　　B. This truth brings _____.
　　C. This truth put our focus on _____.
　　D. This truth challenges us to do an _____
　　　of our lives.

IS THE END NEAR???

Well we close now and in Revelation chapter 20 tells us that there will be a forceful _____ of Satan, a future _____ of the Savior, a final _____ of sinners, and a fixed _____ of sin.

APPLICATION:

_____

_____

_____

_____

_____

ACTION:

_____

_____

_____

IS THE END NEAR???

CHAPTER EIGHT

THE CITY OF GLORY

Revelation 21-22:1-5

1. THE _____ OF HEAVEN.

2. THE _____ OF HEAVEN.

3. THE _____ OF HEAVEN.

   A. The _____ of the City.

   B. The _____ of the City.

   C. The _____ of the City.

   D. The _____ of the City.

4. THE _____ OF HEAVEN.

5. THE _____ OF HEAVEN.

   A. A Place of _____.

   B. A Place of _____.

   C. A Place of _____.

   D. A Place of _____.

IS THE END NEAR???

APPLICATION:
_____
_____
_____
_____
_____
_____
_____
_____

ACTION:
_____
_____
_____
_____

CHAPTER NINE

WHERE IS ISRAEL IN BIBLE PROPHECY?

I. PROPHECIES CONCERNING ISRAEL:

    A. The regathering of the Jews from the _____ _____ of the earth (Isaiah 11:10-12).

    B. The _____ of the state of Israel (Ezekiel 37:21-22).

    C. The _____ of the land (Ezekiel 36:34-35).

    D. The _____ of the Hebrew language (Zephaniah 3:9 and Jeremiah 31:23).

    E. The _____ of the city of Jerusalem (Zechariah 8:4-8).

    F. The _____ of the Israeli military (Zechariah 12:6).

    G. The re-focusing of _____ _____ on the nation of Israel and its city of Jerusalem (Zechariah 12:2-3).

IS THE END NEAR???

II. MILITARY POWER IN PROPHECY:

    A. The War of _____
    (November 1947 – March 1949).

    B. The _____ _____ War (June 1967).

    C. The _____ _____ War (October 1973).

    D. Operation _____ (July 1976).

    E. Operation _____ (June 1981).

III. THE JEWS IN END TIME BIBLE PROPHECY:

1. Prophecies Currently Being Fulfilled.

    A. The Jewish people will be regathered in _____ from the four corners of the earth (Isaiah 11:11-12). Fulfillment: 21st Century and continuing.

    B. The state of Israel will be re-established (Isaiah 66:7-8 & Ezekiel 37:21-22). Fulfillment: _____.

IS THE END NEAR???

    C. The Jews will once again re-occupy the city of Jerusalem (Zechariah 8:4-8), Fulfillment: _____.

    D. The land of Israel will be reclaimed from its desolation, becoming once again a land of agricultural abundance (Ezekiel 36:34-35) Fulfillment: _____ _____.

    E. The Hebrew language will be revived from the dead (Zephaniah 3:9). Fulfillment: _____.

    F. All the nations of the world will come together against Israel over the issue of the control of Jerusalem (Zechariah 12:1-3). Fulfillment: _____ _____.

2. Prophecies _____.

    A. The _____ _____ of the world will attack Israel in a coordinated effort to annihilate the state (Psalm 83).

    B. Israel will soundly defeat the Arab _____ (Zechariah 12:6).

IS THE END NEAR???

C. Israel will dwell in _____ and _____ (Ezekiel 38:11).

D. A Russian coalition consisting mainly of _____ nations will invade Israel (Ezekiel 38:1-17).

E. The _____ coalition will be destroyed supernaturally by God (Ezekiel 38:18-23 & 39:1-8).

F. The _____ will intervene and guarantee the security of Israel, enabling the Jews to rebuild their Temple (Daniel 9:27).

G. At the end of three and a half years, the Antichrist will enter the rebuilt Temple in Jerusalem and _____ himself to be God (Daniel 9:27, Matthew 24:15-18, & 2 Thessalonians 2:3-4).

H. The Jews will reject the Antichrist, and he will respond with an attempt to _____ them, killing two-thirds of them in the process (Revelation 12:13-17 & Zechariah 13:8-9).

IS THE END NEAR???

I. At the end of the Tribulation, when the Jews have come to the end of themselves, they will _____ to God and receive Yeshua as their Messiah (Zechariah 12:10, Romans 9:27-28, & Romans 11:25-27).

J. Jesus will return and regather all _____ Jews to Israel (Deuteronomy 30:1-9).

K. Israel will be established as the _____ nation in the world (Isaiah 2:1-4 & Micah 4:1-7).

L. The Lord will bless the Jewish remnant by _____ all the promises He has made to Israel (Isaiah 60:1-62:7).

M. The blessings of God will flow out to all the nations through the Jewish people during the _____ rule of Jesus (Zechariah 8:22-23).

IS THE END NEAR???

3. Prophecies Concerning the Church.

We will then return with the Lord to this earth (Revelation 19:14), and we will reign with Him for a thousand years (Revelation 20:1-6). During that glorious reign, we will see the earth flooded with peace, righteousness and justice, as the waters cover the seas (Isaiah 11:1-9).

Maranatha!
Come quickly, Lord Jesus!

IS THE END NEAR???

APPLICATION:

_____
_____
_____
_____
_____
_____
_____

ACTIONS:

_____
_____
_____
_____
_____
_____
_____

IS THE END NEAR???

CHAPTER TEN

REVELATION OF THE MAN OF SIN OR SATAN'S SUPERMAN:

1. The _____ of God is _____.

   There's coming one who will sit in the temple of God showing himself that he is God.

2. Not only is the mockery of God recounted, but the _____ of iniquity is _____.

3. The ministry of the Spirit will be _____.

4. The _____ of Satan is _____.

5. I want you to notice, the misery of man is _____.

6. The _____ of Jesus is _____.

IS THE END NEAR???

APPLICATION:

_____
_____
_____
_____
_____
_____
_____

ACTION:

_____
_____
_____
_____

IS THE END NEAR???

NOTES:

CONSLUSION

Why should we care?

_____
_____
_____
_____
_____
_____

What do we do now?

_____
_____
_____
_____
_____
_____

IS THE END NEAR???

Dr. Gene Schuyler

is the Author of the following books:

Total Surrender

Walking by Faith

The Scarlet Thread of Redemption

Give Me An Old Shoe

Creeping Black Mold

God bless you as you walk closer to your Lord and Saviour.
(GS)

www.ingramcontent.com/pod-product-compliance
Lightning Source LLC
Chambersburg PA
CBHW070314230426
43663CB00011B/2126